PROBLEMS IN MODERN EDUCATION

T0370951

PROBLEMS IN MODERN EDUCATION

Edited by

E. D. LABORDE, Ph.D.

Assistant Master at Harrow School

CAMBRIDGE

AT THE UNIVERSITY PRESS

1939

CAMBRIDGE
UNIVERSITY PRESS

University Printing House, Cambridge CB2 8BS, United Kingdom

Published in the United States of America by Cambridge University Press, New York

Cambridge University Press is part of the University of Cambridge.

It furthers the University's mission by disseminating knowledge in the pursuit of
education, learning and research at the highest international levels of excellence.

www.cambridge.org
Information on this title: www.cambridge.org/9781107673991

© Cambridge University Press 1939

First published 1939
First paperback edition 2014

A catalogue record for this publication is available from the British Library

ISBN 978-1-107-67399-1 Paperback

CONTENTS

FOREWORD

THIS volume contains most of the addresses given at the Conference of Young Public School Masters held at Harrow in January, 1938. As on previous occasions, the Committee had arranged a series of lectures on a chosen theme. These have been placed together in Part I and are preceded by a short explanatory address by the Secretary of the Conference, Mr T. F. Coade. They may be said to contain the schoolmaster's 'recall to religion', and the names of the lecturers is a sufficient guarantee of their authority. The unanimity of feeling among men of such different character and experience is impressive and convincing. After the political crisis through which we have just passed, the words of Sir Cyril Norwood sound like those of a prophet of old. Part II contains lectures on different aspects of education, the very variety of which makes any kind of sequence such as will be noticed in Part I impossible. Their character will certainly refute the charges of those persons who sometimes assert that the public schools are unreceptive of new ideas and out of date. It has been found possible to include in an Appendix the main portions of Mr A. C. Cameron's interesting and informative address which opened to many of his hearers a new field of education.

It will be noticed that the book contains none of the authoritative technical lectures included in former collections of addresses delivered at previous Conferences. This is because the purely technical work of the Conference this year was carried out in small sectional gatherings presided over by certain of H.M. Inspectors of Schools who were good enough to consent to guide these discussions. This new arrangement was rendered necessary by the demands of the specialists to whom reference is made by Mr Duckworth in his summary of the progress of secondary education since 1910.

Professor Clarke's address was first delivered at the Conference of the New Ideals in Education at Oxford in 1937.

The lecturer had intended to speak to the Harrow Conference on a different subject, but, owing to a serious illness was unable to complete his intended address. He therefore consented to allow the address included here to be printed instead. The Editor is indebted to the Committee of the New Ideals Conference for permission to reproduce what has already been printed in the report of their Oxford Conference.

The thanks of the Conference are due to the Head Master of Harrow, who once again placed the School buildings at the disposal of the Committee, and to those housemasters who kindly housed the members.

E. D. L.

Harrow-on-the-Hill, 1938

PART I
CHRISTIANITY IN EDUCATION

INTRODUCTORY ADDRESS

T. F. Coade

THE main theme for the Fourth Conference for Young Public School Masters was 'The Educational, Social, and International Relevance of Christianity in the Modern World'. This was intended not so much to attract a large attendance as to challenge as many serious-minded young schoolmasters as possible to face a problem that is becoming increasingly difficult for the public schools. We schoolmasters, like other men, once we have secured comfortable jobs, are sometimes reluctant to face uncomfortable challenges. And the problem presented at this Conference was one which most Englishmen (including schoolmasters) are tempted either to shelve or to regard through spectacles coloured by some prejudice or other.

The issue is plain. Public schools profess and call themselves Christian institutions and claim to be training Christians. At the same time it is becoming more and more difficult in the modern world to know how a Christian should behave or think, notably, for example, in such major contingencies as war, or in the problems of economic equity. How are schoolmasters to guide youth unless they face these problems squarely and courageously themselves? We cannot in this matter fall back on the Englishman's habitual refuge, compromise. In certain contexts compromise is not only permissible but essential. In problems, however, which bring us up against eternal values, in problems which concern religion, a tendency to compromise is not a source of strength but of weakness. And though the present foreign policy of this country seems calculated to postpone war, no one can help feeling that it is based on expediency rather than on any positive constructive faith or theory of life. Is there anything but religion that can introduce this positive constructive spirit into our public or private life?

We shall not awaken a new spirit in the youth of this
country by merely decrying the attitude and behaviour of
the great totalitarian states. Youth in these states has reached
a far more splendid and dynamic consciousness of what life
might be than we have. They are inspired by a far greater
enthusiasm, devotion, and readiness for service than most
young people in this country. The tragedy of their idealisms
is that they contain the seeds of their own inevitable failure,
just because their leaders have misunderstood the real nature
of man: they are in too great a hurry to achieve the millen-
nium. In order to hasten things on, they over-stimulate
those human qualities which will further the immediate
ends of nationalism; but in order to do this certain fundamental and often more important human qualities are sup-
pressed. While it lasts, this way of life raises them to a degree
of heroism and self-devotion which we might well envy.
But how long will it last? It is precisely here that Christianity
provides a solution, if we could only see it. For Christ
demanded the devotion of the whole man—all his faculties,
human and divine, in the service of God and of the whole of
humanity. It is only the sense that he has devoted himself to
that service that can bring to man freedom and peace. Any
ideal that is less than that, e.g. where dictators have to whip
up antagonism against other groups in order to keep alive
the enthusiasm of their followers, is bound sooner or later
to fail and leave men in a worse state than that from which
they started. At any time in history, and especially at the
present time, no conception of human relationships that does
not aim at universal co-operation and brotherhood can
settle anything on a permanent basis. What we need in this
country is to awaken in youth the same enthusiasm and
readiness for service as we find in totalitarian states, but
enable them to relate it to the Christian ideal and the Christian
way of life. That we cannot do until we have begun to find
that way and live that life ourselves.

THE EDUCATIONAL, SOCIAL, AND INTERNATIONAL RELEVANCE OF CHRISTIANITY IN THE MODERN WORLD

Cyril Norwood

THOUGH in the course of this book others will discuss, more fully than I can, the question 'What is Christianity?' I feel that for the sake of clearness I must try and give a provisional answer myself. I hold the essence of Christianity to be this, that God is real, that the spiritual values are real, and that a future existence is real, even though none of these propositions is capable of what we call exact scientific proof. Further, that at a definite period of historic time God became man, manifested Himself in the life of the human Jesus, to show to mankind the Way of Life. There are many forms and varieties of opinion under which we can hold fast to these essential truths, but I do not regard any particular form or variety of dogma as essential, so long as these central propositions are accepted. It is the relevance of this faith to the modern world in its educational, social, and international aspects with which I propose to deal in broad outline.

It is to be observed first of all that its truth and validity are openly challenged and denied at the present time with a frankness such as has not been known for centuries. The existence of the many who profess the faith with their lips, though their hearts are far from it, has long been known and felt. These we have with us to-day in numbers certainly not less than in former times. But we are also in the presence of an open and avowed Anti-Christ. It is based on the proposition which, though it was not originated by Karl Marx it is convenient to associate with him, that the economic values are alone real, and that on this basis alone can human history be explained and guided with wisdom. The traditions and the mythology of the Christian religion are, it is alleged, in reality a form of dope administered by the possessing classes to the have-nots, to the workers of the world, the rotten and decaying prop of a moribund and decaying system. This is not a theory of the study, but has been translated into action: it has swept away a Church, and destroyed a priesthood and a social order. It has kindled, in the hearts of a considerable number, a fervour comparable to the glowing enthusiasm of a religious faith, and has sent forth thousands of young Russians ardently upon the path of building a social order which shall be free from superstition, and give to all men a sense of freedom and a chance of happiness. It may seem to us an odd delusion. The freedom and the happiness seem to the eyes of most of us not to be there. But to them they are real; for them the dethronement of God and the enthronement in its place of the Soviet Republic represent a happy exchange. We must not under-estimate the reality of it all because we dislike it.

This is, as I see it, only one of the manifestations of the theory of materialism, the belief that the only things that are real are the things which you can see and touch and handle, and take away and make your own. In Germany, in Italy, and in other countries as well, Caesar sits enthroned in the place of God, and the state is offered to the eyes of the nations as the exclusive object of worship. Hitler and Mussolini, in a sense more universal than ever Louis XIV could aspire to, say to their nationals, "The State, it is I". Hitler for reasons of policy may attack the Roman and the Protestant communions; Mussolini for reasons of policy may keep in with the Roman Church. But there is no difference between the two theories. Again the only real values are economic, and the world presents itself as a storehouse of economic wealth, God and a moral order are a delusion, an outworn tradition: there is no such thing as eternal life. Therefore we must concentrate on the things which really matter, and, since the world's wealth is limited, it is obvious that the wise will make themselves strong enough to get the lion's portion in the share-out. God and the moral order being ruled out, all must depend upon power: 'for why? the good old rule sufficeth them, the simple plan, that they should take who have the power, and they should keep who can.' Hence the state in the pursuit of its destiny may lie, rob, steal, murder, so long as it is justified by success, and there is only too much in history which gives warrant to this theory of politics.

But to me the important aspect of the whole case is that it presents itself to the young German, to the young Italian, as a release, honour from disgrace, light from darkness, power from weakness; it captures his imagination, it enlists all the ardours of youth, it offers him the chance of a glorious self-sacrifice, escape from the sordid and the commonplace, the sublimation of self. We cannot understand their frame of mind; we too suffered in the war, and learned the horrors that result from militant and competitive materialism. But we won the war; we did not go through the valley of conscious weakness, suffering, and dishonour, when those nations felt that there could be no God. There is no God, they said, but Germany shall be great, Italy shall be great. The individual matters not at all, only the greatness, the grandeur, the glory, the power, the might that the state will achieve. The true liberty is to combine, to build up the force that shall prove itself irresistible, when the earth shall be ours and the fulness thereof. Again in this Nazism, this Fascism, we catch the religious note, the fervour that can make men greater than themselves. Nothing great is done without enthusiasm, and the enthusiasm is undoubtedly there.

Granted the premises, it all seems to me to be perfectly logical. Cancel out God, dismiss Christ as a myth, His teaching as a delusion, and the rest seems to follow. Make yourselves strong, sharpen your swords, and take what you want. Granted the premises, it deserves its title of 'Real

Politics'. We can approach its believers and say, I think with truth: 'This sounds all very well, but it leads Europe over the precipice.' We have fought one world-war for power, wealth, and influence, and it left us bled white and deadly weak, miserably poor, and without a shred of influence. These material values are not real: they perish under our hands while we fight for them. This policy can only lead to the decadence of the nations, the twilight of Europe, possibly a new dark age. But they turn deaf ears to us. It will not be so bad as we pretend, because of our weakness, that it is going to be. We, the western democracies, are fat degenerates, sagging with our ill-gotten wealth: we profess a hypocritical religion, we maintain a hypocritical social and political system. We are pacifists, because we are afraid. Britain, for instance, as the lecturers at times say in their discourses on the colonies to Germans, is a country where the grandfathers knew how to create an empire, and the fathers knew how to hold it, but the sons will lose it, because they dare not and will not fight for it. It is fruit hanging on the trees, to be had for the picking.

The simplest way to argue with a man who has reached this state of mind is to hit him on the nose, because this is the only argument which he will understand. But that way madness lies. That in a nutshell is the difficulty of the present international situation.

There is another attack on Christianity and its values which comes from the side of what is popularly known as modern psychology. Modern psychology speaks with many voices and is trying out a number of inconsistent theories. But it is popularly supposed, in some self-styled intellectual circles, that God has been explained away as a wish-phantasy, or, alternatively, as a Father-complex, or, alternatively, as a projection of the personality: in any case He is not real. Of necessity therefore there can be no reality in prayer, and so there must be a totally different valuation of morality. Conscience disappears, sin cannot exist in any real sense.

A man may hold these views in Britain, France, or America, and act as a solvent of the structure of society: he will follow his self-interest, enlightened or unenlightened, and will not fulfil his social obligations unless it clearly pays him so to do. If he holds these views in Germany or Italy or Russia, and goes so far as to act up to them, he will find himself either segregated or liquidated. He can of course call God what he likes: but if he calls the state a wish-phantasy, in spite of the much more genuine grounds that he has for doing so than in the case of God, he would soon be in a concentration camp, or cutting logs in Siberia. I do not wish to elaborate this side of our subject, but only to illustrate what is a very relevant fact, that the democracies are open to every kind of dis-integrating influence and factious self-interest, all making for obvious weakness, and the totalitarian states have crushed all this sort of thing out of existence, or driven it underground, so making for apparent strength.

Here then is Anti-Christ, no vague theoretic danger, but present and capable of destroying or darkening the life of everybody in this country. What weapon have we for meeting this peril? first and strongest of all, I think, education. The strength and temper of this weapon are well understood in the totalitarian states, for it is directed firmly to its purpose, the turning out of good Communists, Fascists, or Nazis. It is not enough to call this an education in blinkers, and to be content with an education of our own, which is not directed to any particular end, and leaves all the important issues that condition our lives as so many open questions. If they can produce young men and women who are, within their limits, genuine idealists, then must we produce men and women more enlightened, but not less devoted. It is in connection with this issue that the educational relevance of Christianity in the modern world most justly engages our attention.

We have a theory, inherited from the nineteenth century and bred by the age-long sectarian strife of Christians, that there is such a thing as secular education, an education which can properly leave out God, and have nothing to say of Time and Eternity. It is vaguely supposed that information on these grave issues will be given at home, or in the churches. However, such teaching has ceased to be given in the homes, and the pupils do not attend the churches: hence we are breeding a population that is predominantly pagan, which believes that education is merely a process which prepares you for an examination, in order that you may get a job. People generally are beginning to be uneasy and even distressed, because there appears to be something lacking in this education. But they have not yet grasped that education is a preparation for life, and the consequences which flow from this truth.

I have not long come home from a journey in which I had occasion to lecture on education in most of the chief cities of New Zealand and Australia. There they have educational systems sharply and clearly defined by law, as free, compulsory, and secular, which means in other and less resounding words that the pupils go to school to cram up the subjects which will enable them to pass an external examination. The teachers are profoundly dissatisfied, but have yet to grasp the fundamental truth that religion and education are so bound together that they are in their development two sides of one process. For an education which is wholly secular is an education which declares in effect that God does not matter, and that the spiritual values are of no importance for life. In this issue there can be no compromise, and he that is not with me is against me. It is a modern delusion to think that you can safely leave this question open, and that it is in the spirit of modern progress to leave the minds of children unbiased so that they can decide for themselves. This is in effect to teach them that those particular considerations do not matter. You do not leave them, or think of leaving them, unbiased as to the laws which govern their bodily health: that is an action which would obviously be

absurd. Why is it not as obviously absurd to let them grow
up ignorant of all that concerns their spiritual health? the
meaning of this life, their place in the world?

The answer will be, because we have no certainty, and as
soon as you try to introduce this sort of teaching, all the
schools and churches fly at each others' throats. But is this
true? Here are two clear-cut issues about life. Let me re-
capitulate. On the one hand it is said that God is a delusion,
and that prayer is a delusion. You are, here, an animal in a
material world, and the only real values are material. You
are part of a nation that must make itself strong enough to
secure the place in the sun which belongs to it by right,
because it is potentially strong enough to take it and to keep
it. On the other hand it is said that these values are only
apparently real: they are transitory. Reality is spiritual, and
each one of us is a spirit. Our values are spiritual: they are
truth, beauty, and goodness. It is possible to gain the whole
world, and to lose one's own soul; and it is not worth it.
Turn away from that region of material values where you
can only gain by your neighbour's losses, and where the values
themselves perish while you fight for them; and turn rather
to that spiritual kingdom where the values increase by being
shared, where your own share of truth and goodness and beauty
makes that of everyone else so much the greater and the
more possible, where the kingdom in which God is revealed
is love, and love is made perfect by sacrifice. If this is true,
can we reasonably or safely leave it out of education? is it not
vital to right living? is it not a far nobler, even if admittedly
a more difficult ideal than that other, to which by a merely
secular education we by our very silence condemn the generation, whom it is our duty to prepare fully for life? And this,
as I see it, is but another way of saying that other foundation
can no man lay than that is laid, even Jesus Christ.

The claim that I am making is, therefore, that national
education ought to be frankly based on Christianity conceived of in this broad spirit. If it is true, it is the most

valuable of all the truths which we have to impart to those that come after us. In what way can it be imparted? Christianity, thought of thus, thought of as the first Christians thought of it, is a way of life, and that way of life must be followed in the school, giving light and warmth both to corporate and to individual living. Instruction there must be, and I will say a word on it presently. But far more important than the actual instruction is it that the whole school should feel itself to be a social organism in miniature, made up on the part of masters and boys by individual wills freely co-operating, and feeling their truest freedom, their fullest self-expression, in so doing. It should be felt to be a life lived to a common end, a society formed to bring out the best in each individual, and yet so inspired that the individual seeks to give his best in return to the common life. Just as in the Christian gospel we are expressly bidden to 'render unto Caesar the things which are Caesar's, and unto God the things that are God's', never merging the value of the human soul in the mere service of the state, and yet providing always that each individual human soul shall find its full development through service to others in and through the state, so the school should be equally balanced and equally true in its estimates of comparative values. The Archbishop of York once said that there was no reason why even an elementary school should not constitute itself as a church in miniature: I think that this carries us too far on the road to an artificial self-consciousness, but it has its foundation of truth. There is no reason why every school should not feel itself to be a spiritual adventure taken in common, a life to which each has something individual, something of his own, to contribute, a life quickened by example, whose inspiration passes, like the flame of the torch, from a life to a life.

And the teachers should be more sensible than they are that their calling is a vocation. They will not have done all their task if they have merely been adequate in their teaching of Quadratic Equations or the rules of Oratio Obliqua. They have indeed to know what they want their boys to know, but they have also to be, and they ought to be, what they want their boys to be. There is a life of example to be lived by every schoolmaster worthy of the name.

There must be religious instruction also, a task of which many schools make heavy weather. The time is very limited: it is easy to say that the home and the church should be responsible for most of the actual knowledge to be gained. But as I have already said, for different reasons neither source can be depended on, and it is astonishing how ignorant boys from good and even cultured homes can be. There is therefore a definite task laid upon the school to give a considered course of instruction, and in most schools there are far too few who are qualified to give it. To teach clearly what I conceive to be necessary, viz. the progressive revelation of God in the Old Testament, the Manifestation of the Divine Nature in Jesus, the teachings of the Gospel; to put this forward clearly, in the light of modern criticism, needs a teacher who is well read and understands the position which he has to establish and maintain. I think therefore that the teaching should be mainly in the hands of specialists. I wish that it were not so, for in following this course something is lost from the universality of its appeal. But it does require a scholar, by which I mean a person who has gone through a regular course of preparatory study, to put forward Christian teaching on a firm foundation, and we can no longer expect such a thorough preparation from everybody.

I hold also that every school should, as a school, engage in some piece of social work, something over which each individual boy has a chance of taking personal trouble. We do not want merely the sort of enterprise which is satisfied by a vicarious half-crown, or a silver collection on a special Sunday. So it may be a boys' club, it may be scouting, it may be work for the unemployed, it may be a service of beautifying or protecting the countryside, it may be a score of things. But the important thing is that the social goodwill that is fostered in the school should issue in action; that the boys should do something, and should learn by example not to be content unless they have a share in that something which is being done. This side of school activity needs a constant watchfulness, for it so easily becomes conventional and traditional, as indeed has been the case with so many of the School Missions which were started with bright hopes at the end of last century, and are now lifeless.

If we turn to the social relevance of Christianity, we are in a field of infinite speculation and variety. I must of necessity be summary in my method. Jesus did not come on earth to advocate a political creed, to preach a political revolution, or to reform the world by political action of any sort. He was content, in the words I have already quoted, to bid men 'render unto Caesar the things that are Caesar's, and unto God the things that are God's'. So far as I can tell, He bade those who sought to make the world better to go away and make themselves better. He was quite frankly anthropomorphic in His teaching, taught that God was a loving Father, that we were His children, and He taught us how to pray as little children at a father's knee. I think that this is important to remember and to reflect upon, for even if the Christian view of Him be mistaken, He was the greatest religious genius that the world has ever known, and He was not in the least afraid of thinking in these simple forms, even though He may have said that God is a spirit, and they that worship Him must worship in spirit and in truth. He relied on gradualness, on the change wrought in many individual hearts, on the change wrought by many individuals following Him. His favourite metaphor, or one of His favourite metaphors, was that of the leaven leavening the lump. He did not mind apparent failure, if this was the immediate fruit of a loyal following of the ideal. He may, or may not, have expected a speedy end to the world, a coming of God in power, a vindication of the chosen people. If He did, He attempted nothing political to bring it about.

Has this any relevance for the modern world? I think that it has. We have seen a great deal of what is called social progress, and there is no doubt that from a material point of view the world is a much more comfortable place for the poor man, and his children have a much better chance, than ever they had in the past. It all seems to have flowed from the awakening of the social conscience, and there can be no question that the awakening of that social conscience was due to the influence of the Christian ethic. Let us run over in our minds its main features: the abolition of slavery, for which our own country was ready to barter definite material interests; the growth of the great hospital services on a voluntary basis, the protection of the young from excessive hours of labour, the protection of women, the care for old age, the protection against accident, and against illness, the protection against unemployment. The names of prominent Christian leaders in these causes come to the mind: men like Shaftesbury, Wilberforce, women like Florence Nightingale, Elizabeth Fry; but they had with them and behind them a great flowing tide of Christian opinion, which was ready and willing to translate into political reality the old Christian rule, that a man should seek to love his brother as himself. There was political theory at work as well, and I am of course not denying it; but what made the engine of reform work so easily was the genuine Christianity which was in the hearts of the people, the ordinary folk from church and chapel. And so without strife or civil bloodshed we have been transformed in this country from a privileged oligarchy to an unrestricted democracy: we have accepted heavy taxation, if not without complaint, at any rate without disloyal resistance: our country is worth living in, just because at bottom it is still Christian. The lump has been partly leavened.

The process has been called slow, hypocritical, unreal, by the vendors of revolutions and of political quick-cures.

Well, we have had some object lessons from the results and the history of revolutions. We have seen how true it is that revolution devours its own children, and seldom waits long before doing so. The French Revolution passed rapidly through a Reign of Terror into a military autocracy: it did a great work indeed, but at a great price in human suffering and bloodshed. In the country of its origin it left behind a tradition of violence which flowered again in the Paris Commune: its class hatreds still continue, and may at any moment blossom again into civil war. The Bolshevik revolution has been a still grimmer story, in part, for the reason, in my opinion, that there was much less Christian faith and idealism to dilute it. It put whole classes of a whole nation to death, dishonour, and degradation. It has turned upon its own authors and has staged a continent-wide Reign of Terror. It has thrown overboard its old ideals, such as they were, and has become a tyranny of the familiar sort. Russians may be happier than they were, for by our standards they were in old days very miserable. But by our standards they are still miserable. The great revolution has not been a short way to a new Heaven and a new earth.

War and revolution solve no problems, right no wrongs: they only substitute another set of wrongs for those which previously existed. The Christian view is that these material things, votes, wages, political power, are not of the first order of importance, not the main concern of life, which is right living, or doing the Will of Our Father in Heaven. But 'seek ye first the kingdom of God, and all these things will be added unto you'. Has anyone ever shown that to be false and unfounded? It is the literal truth. We may call ourselves Tories, and if we are Christian Tories, we shall try and improve the lot of the people. We may call ourselves Labour, and if there is any Christianity in our Labour Politics, our first concern will be to improve the lot of the people. And there will not be a lot of difference between us, when the history of, let us say, fifty years comes to be written. We shall always differ, but if we are at the bottom of us Christian, our differences will illuminate each the other. Let us therefore listen to every man who is insistent to teach us what he has found true in his own experience. Let us turn deaf ears to the man who is crying aloud that his neighbour is wrong. Let us try to follow the man who is trying to construct and to build: let us turn away from the man who seeks to pull down and destroy. Class hatred is a sorry thing, and can make no foundation for a nation or a living human society. Communism in its true form is centuries away: you cannot introduce the reign of love by blood and terror. When malice and hatred exist let us try to take away the causes, remembering our own danger, if we are born in the comfortable classes, of becoming sleek and insensitive, remembering, too, that the New Testament has many things disquieting to say to the rich, and a good deal to comfort the poor. It does not tell them, however, to liquidate the rich, or to rob them either on the highway or at the polling booth. I do not see how anyone can doubt that in education, in the spread of what are known as the social services, in the conduct of industry and commerce, and the management of employment, the Spirit of Christianity is not bound to be our best guide. We have tried 'Laissez faire' and have done with it: we no longer have any belief in the virtues of unrestricted competition. We are trying slowly, half-heartedly if you like, methods which are, at bottom, Christian in their inspiration: the policy of the good neighbour. Let us go on with these methods and never be tempted to think that, by this or by that short cut and quick and violent application of any materialist political theory, we are going to find ourselves at the particular haven where we would be.

When we turn to international affairs, Christianity, which seems to be regarded by a large part of the world as entirely irrelevant, appears on any just view to be more relevant, if possible, than it is anywhere else. But strait is the way and narrow the gate, and few there be that find it. I have already said a certain amount upon this aspect of our subject, and I will only take three topics to illustrate what I mean. There are two views that may be taken of colonies; the first one is at any rate justified by the tradition of centuries, but it is a tradition which many hoped that the world had outgrown. Cicero, long ago, called the provinces of Rome 'praedia populi Romani', estates of the Roman people, estates to be exploited for the benefit of the possessing nation. Spain lost an empire by a too literal acceptance of that theory, and so did we. It came to be held in the nineteenth century that this theory did not apply to provinces inhabited by the white races, but it continued to apply to those which were tenanted by the backward and the dark. Then in this century a different conception gained ground, which is enshrined in the system of Mandates, under the tutelage of the League of Nations, that such territories are to be administered for the benefit of their inhabitants, and that the duty of the controlling power is to develop, educate, and protect, with the ultimate object of giving freedom and independence. This then constitutes a second and totally different view of colonies. It is not accepted by the totalitarian states; to Germany and to Italy colonies are estates held for their own benefit and for their own exclusive trade, nor is any other conception accepted in Japan. That appears to me to be the whole difficulty in meeting in any way Germany's demand for the restoration of her colonies, since that demand puts the clock back definitely, excludes the conception of a trust, and reverts in the crudest manner to the conception which it was hoped that the world had outgrown. I should myself see with pleasure the whole of Central Africa for instance, put under international control, in the spirit of a mandate, with free access for all nations to the raw materials which that region can produce. But I should not see with pleasure, the same territory divided into fenced-off areas, and each with its notice, 'Trespassers will be prosecuted', each being exploited in the interests of the commerce of its owners.

The Mandate policy is difficult and may seem to a European country to cost more trouble than it is worth. But it is right: it is a genuine piece of the good neighbour policy which Christianity inculcates. It will be a thousand pities if, like other ideals born of the ideals of our religion, it is rendered impossible by the selfishness and jealousy of nations.

Then in the economic sphere there is the whole doctrine of the self-sufficiency of nations, based on the crazy idea that you can and ought to sell to other nations, but that you need not buy from them; and on another crazy idea, that you can be prosperous and rich when the rest of the world of your rivals is poor and in distress. The natural result has followed that international trade now flows in a thin and shallow stream, and it has become a commonplace with economists to say that there can be no real recovery until the stream of international trade is restored to its old volume. I take it that the progress of communications in speed and in certainty, the conquest of natural forces by science, the ability to bring need and supply into instantaneous touch, all point logically to the next step, when the world economically will be a single community, and all seas be open and all roads free. In such a world there should and could be, universal free trade, a high standard of living, and leisure, culture, and health. But it all lies for the present in the land of dreams. The gates that lead on to that road are locked and double locked by the process which makes for economic national-ism. It is said to be patriotic for us each to look after our-selves and let our neighbours do the same. But it is not Christian: it offers comfort for the moment but no hope for the future.

It is, however, but one side of the process of which we are unwilling witnesses, the process by which Europe, forgetful of all the lessons of the war, has become a camp of jealously watchful nations more heavily armed than ever. I am not going to speak much of the League of Nations, which for its primary and more important purpose lies like a machine mutilated and wrecked. Every consideration of Christianity and of commonsense points to the League method as being the right way. But you cannot move a step on that way when you cannot trust your neighbour's word, and dare not even turn your back on him without looking all the time over your shoulder. There is nothing more certain than that the maintenance of vast armed forces will sooner or later lead to their employment by some ambitious fool or knave, nothing surer than that such action will bring in its train poverty, misery, and ruin and will deprive Europe of its place in the march of civilisation. Yet we go on, and the horror of the situation is that we cannot help going on. You cannot be much more moral than your neighbours. If you had to live all your days in the company of burglars and assassins, you would not live a life of so high a moral tone as if you were living, let us say, in a society of young public-school masters. But that is the position in Europe to-day. We are living with people who may at any moment, if they think that it will pay them, knock us on the head. We are constantly told that there is a conflict between two idealogies, those of Fascism and Bolshevism, and we are urged to look at Spain, where both sides are fishing in the witch's cauldron which they have helped to brew. The conflict lies deeper and concerns us much more closely: it concerns Christianity much more closely. It is the conflict between democracy and authoritarianism, between freedom and compulsion, liberty and despotism. It is not for nothing that Mussolini, the frankest, the most unashamed, the most tactless and the most vocal, of the dictators hurls his insults at western democracy, on almost all occasions when he opens his mouth in public, or puts pen to paper. And the basic fact is this, that democracy is capable of being a Christian conception, and along its roads Christian ideas and ideals can work themselves out harmoniously, but in the totalitarian state they cannot.

At bottom it depends upon the conception which you have

formed of human personality. Is the human personality of value in itself? am I a child of God and an heir to eternal life, as Christianity teaches? Then if that be the case the state exists ultimately for me and for others like me: it establishes and maintains the conditions under which we shall have the best chance of living a good life, in the Aristotelian sense if you like, in the Christian sense as I prefer. In this light we can interpret life, liberty, and the pursuit of happiness, which are the Right of Man; in this light we can interpret Liberty, Fraternity, and Equality, which can be Christian ideals through and through. You can, if you like, make endless fun of democracy as a political system; but what Mussolini and his fellow critics do not understand is that democracy is more than a political system: it is a social system, it is a way of life. Where liberty exists, there is a general will, and a general will which, if it is based on an enlightened education and a real basis of religion, makes itself felt and is strong enough to give some reality to the rhetorical phrase of Lincoln: 'Government of the people by the people, for the people.' Cut away liberty and freedom of the spirit from education and there is no such thing as enlightened general will. The vigour of life is gone out of the social organism. The individual steadily relapses into a life in which he is in himself of no value, and which will inevitably become for him poor and nasty, brutish and short. That is the great issue for the future of humanity which has to be fought out in this century. There is just a chance, but it is a slight chance, that it will not have to be fought out in a literal sense. Reason may prevail, but who shall penetrate to the ears that are made deaf, and the eyes that are blindfolded, and through the barrage of lies which compasses the nations round about?

Religion and education can alone help the world, and if I am right in the course of thought which I have put before you, religion and education can no longer be separated, and there is no higher vocation than that which falls to the schoolmaster. For they work in the service of a great hope. If there can be given to the democracies of Europe and of the United States, through education, a common basis of thought, and a common background, and a broad common ideal, there is enough power, enough wealth, enough population to sway the future of the world. But if democracy is not ennobled by religion, it will not survive, and if the Christian values cease to have honour among men, then will perish with them not only the reality of progress, but the possibility of hope.

WHAT IS CHRISTIANITY?

W. R. Inge

'THE Relevance of Christianity'—the title of an excellent book by Canon Barry—is a most interesting, important and comprehensive subject. And we can't even begin to discuss it till we make it clear to ourselves and others what we mean by Christianity, a vaguer word than Conservatism, Liberalism, and Socialism, which is saying a great deal.

Christianity is the collective name in use for the religions professed by people with white skins, if they have any religion at all. It has taken almost every form which a religion can take. It began as a revival of prophetic religion within Judaism. Prophetic religion was antisacerdotal, usually non-political, personal, moral, and spiritual. These were notably the characteristics of the Galilean ministry. Detaching itself from the Palestinian Church, which had not much hold over the Jewish Diaspora, Christianity, guided by St Paul, entered the field of Hellenistic civilisation, and became a mystery religion, a cult of *Kyrios Christos*, but refusing any concession to the popular Theocrasia. It retained from its Palestinian origin an exclusive monotheism, a slowly fading hope in a catastrophic divine apocalypse in the near future, and an eschatology which, though mainly Platonic, did not cut itself loose from time and place, and emphasised personality and retribution more than Greek thought as a whole cared to do. It defined its position against Manichean dualism which had its source in Persia, against Gnostic theosophy, against syncretistic paganism, and against Judaism. It freely adopted most of the current philosophy, which meant that its metaphysics was mainly Platonic, its ethics mainly Stoical. But it was firm about the historical incarnation, about future judgment, and about the creation of the world in time—in these articles of faith it was resolved 'to take time seriously'. But the idea of a long duration of the world, during which humanity was to progress towards perfection as if by an inevitable law or divine decree, was absent both from the Church and its rivals.

The attempts of the Roman Government to suppress the new religion, as an *imperium in imperio*, were sporadic, half-hearted, and futile. They ended in a victory, not so much of the Galilean over Jupiter, as of the Church over the Empire. Henceforth the 'Two Cities' of Augustine's conception stood side by side in uneasy alliance. In the East, the Church was the right arm of the Basileus; in the West, the break up of the Empire put the Pope in a still greater position. The Holy Roman Church, and the Holy German Empire, both claiming *de iure* universality, had the curious result of preventing the unification of Italy and Germany till living memory.

Christianity in the Dark Ages was itself inevitably dark, but on the whole it kept alive some poor relics of the old civilisation, and made society less savage than it would have been otherwise. The lavish gifts of land and money to the Church prove that its work was very highly honoured.

This was the time when asceticism, not originally a Christian movement, and especially the cult of virginity, swept over the Church. The ideal is not yet extinct, and we must make up our minds whether, and to what extent, Christianity, as we use the word, is committed to world-renouncing ideas, and especially to a law of severe sex-repression. In the Synoptic Gospels rigorism and humanism stand side by side, but I do not think it is really difficult to understand the position of the Founder.

Another alien importation, rather later, is of great interest. Chivalry was not indigenous in the Mediterranean lands; it came south with the 'barbarian' invaders. It was accepted by the Church at the time of the Crusades; afterwards it fell into contempt, as we see from Cervantes. On the whole I think it is alien to the Gospel, which does not mean that it was contrary to it. The importance of this movement for our present subject is this. Chivalry survives in the romantic idea of sexual love, and in the ideal character of the gentleman, the lay-religion of the Englishman, especially in our Public Schools. How far are these integral parts of Christianity?

That the Papacy is the heir of the Caesars is no mere clever epigram of Hobbes; it is the truth. The Roman Church is the last chapter in the history of the Roman Empire. We in this country do not think of the *pontifex maximus* on the Vatican when we discuss the relevance of Christianity to modern conditions, but on the Continent the Pope still looms large, as the head of a powerful organisation, the Black International, one of the totalitarian states.

The climax of the Middle Ages as distinguished from the Dark Ages was the almost simultaneous discovery of a new world above us (Copernicus and Galileo), a new world beyond the seas (Columbus and Magellan), and a new world within—the recovery of what could be recovered of the legacy of Greece. The Mediterranean world seemed to be relapsing into paganism, and Northern Europe, which had never been Greek or Roman, had its own Renaissance in the Reformation. Neopaganism in the South gave way to the harsh Counter-Reformation, Spanish not Italian. From that time Southern Europe has been Latin, not Catholic; Northern Europe, after dallying with a return to the Old Testament, has been fumbling for a religion which should really express its spirit.

The most characteristic of these developments in Northern Europe was Calvinism or Puritanism, in which Christianity for the first time came to terms with secular civilisation in what was to be its modern form. Hitherto, Catholicism had been feudal and agrarian. It is still most at home in peasant communities. But Calvinism was urban. Rejecting the dietary rules and disciplinary system of Catholicism, it encouraged an intra-mundane asceticism. The typically godly life consisted in a diligent performance of some useful and productive task. Business was to be strictly honest; there was to be no self-indulgence, no useless and demoralising luxury; no oppression of the worker or swindling of the buyer. Some pleasures, such as the theatre and cardplaying, were frowned upon. All sex-indulgence outside marriage was sternly forbidden. The Sunday was identified with the Jewish Sabbath. *Septima quaeque dies turpi damnata veterno Tamquam lassati mollis imago Dei.*

This ethical programme fitted in almost too well with the ambitions of vigorous expanding nations while there were still new worlds to conquer. Calvinism made the nations which adopted it rich and prosperous. The nineteenth-century business man, if he was not a child of the Ghetto, was a grandson of John Calvin.

The peculiarity of this phase of religion was that there was no questioning of values. Cf. Clough's poem beginning 'Hope evermore and believe'. But when people began to ask " What is the use and the good?"—and the question could not be set aside—the system began to break up from within. Business broke away from religion, and especially from asceticism. The Calvinistic ethos still lingers in North America and Scotland. It is at its best among the Quakers, who have retained their simplicity and zeal in social reforms.

In the eighteenth century there appeared the last of the great heresies—belief in a law of progress and human perfectibility. It began as an acute secularisation of the Christian hope, in the age of rationalism. As the apocalyptic dreams of the first Christians took wings and flew away to the Platonic idea of a supra-mundane heaven, so now they returned to earth as a vision of 'a good time coming'. Very soon these dreams were seized upon by the revolution, which turned them into a kind of religion. A popular religion is a superstition which has enslaved a philosophy. In this case the superstition was belief in a law of progress, the philosophy

was a misunderstanding of the theory of evolution as taught by
Darwin. Of course, Christianity has nothing to say to it. The
early Church believed that the end of the world was very
near, and did not regret it. As late as A.D. 1000 there was a
general expectation that the end was imminent. Roger
Bacon was convinced that Anti-Christ, the precursor of the
final cataclysm, was at the door. Prayers were offered *pro
mora finis*—men felt they were not quite ready. The idea of a
gradual progress of humanity, though not negatived by
Christianity, neither is, nor ever has been, part of the Christian
religion. It is only quite recently that the probability of an
immense vista of years in which the earth will be habitable
has caught hold of the popular imagination. It is an inspiring
thought, and we may regret that we cannot find it in Christian
theology. The classical substitute for it was the law of
cycles—alternate periods of progress and decline. This was
rejected by the Church as interfering with its own eschatology,
but it is not yet obsolete. On a cosmic scale it is an alternative to the depressing law of entropy—that the whole
universe is running down irrevocably like a clock. I find it
difficult to accept this; for it implies that the universe started,
as Eddington says, 'with a bang' at a date which we could
name if we knew it; and this is very hard to believe. Whatever power wound the clock up once may presumably wind
it up again. But whichever theory we choose, the law of
perpetual progress labours under the disadvantage of being
almost the only philosophical theory which can be definitely
disproved.

Puritanism is the last attempt at a Church-directed civilisation. Catholicism has abated none of its claims, and is still
a political force, even in England, where it can intimidate
candidates for Parliament (e.g. on birth-control and eutha-
nasia) and threaten editors and publishers. It can bargain
with governments in a way which the Church of England
cannot. But it can never be more than a well-disciplined
faction. Puritanism is a middle-class creed, the creed of the

patient ass bowed beneath two burdens. Duty and discipline
are not words to conjure with either for the scum or the
dregs of society.

Independently of the Churches there have been quasi-
religious ideals and movements which have been of great
importance in modern civilisation. The idea of Emancipation
has had a long history—a history of victories over kings,
priests, aristocracies, constitutional assemblies, laws, and
customs in restraint of liberty. In the last century most
people believed that the future of liberty in all civilised
countries was assured. But it is checked at once when a
nation is threatened either with foreign conquest or internal
disruption. It is not the strongest form of government.
It postulates a measure of security against foreign attack, and
a fundamental unity at home behind party struggles. These
conditions could be secured if the world were really Christian.
They do not exist in Europe to-day. Beyond this, Christianity has no strong preference for any one form of con-
stitution.

Another characteristic movement of our time is National-
ism. The early Church was accused of 'incivism'; the Roman
Government failed to stimulate keen patriotism among the
Christians by their policy of throwing them to the lions.
But the thought of the coming ruin of his country brought
the rare tears to the eyes of Christ; St Paul was willing to be
'accursed' for the sake of his countrymen. We cannot say
that love of country is not a Christian emotion. But aggressive militarism is absolutely un-Christian. Augustine terms
wars of conquest *magna latrocinia*. So is racialism of the
German type. And of course the same condemnation falls
upon the ambitions of political Churches. *Extra ecclesiam
nulla salus* is the most fundamentally un-Christian maxim
ever uttered. It has been the parent of innumerable crimes
of cruelty and fraud.

A third quasi-religious enthusiasm has arisen out of class
strife. Seditions of this kind have always been common.

They helped to wreck both the civilisation of the Greek city states and the very similar civilisation of medieval Italy. The remedies most widely employed in the past have been slavery—a class of 'animate tools', which in the long run is usually fatal to the slave-owning class; and the caste system, which in India has shown extraordinary strength and toughness. The European experiment of industrialism and capitalism has produced an unparalleled growth of wealth and population, but it demands what the astronomers call an 'expanding universe', and our globe does not expand. The great achievement of modern industrialism is in the progress of applied sciences, labour-saving machinery. In a slave-state it is not worth while to save labour. The new wealth is really created neither by capital nor by labour, but by ingenious inventors who mostly remain poor. If you put a lump of unclaimed honeycomb between two hives, the bees will fight for it till the ground is covered with corpses. So it has been in our societies. The probable solution is an almost complete displacement of manual toil by machinery, which will mean a regulated population and a regulated output.

But the stress of conflicting interests has given birth to a philosophy sometimes called dialectical materialism, and to a rewriting of history with almost exclusive attention to economics. The consistent exponents of this philosophy are fiercely opposed to Christianity, on grounds which I shall presently explain; and Catholicism on its side proclaims that there can be no reconciliation of this quarrel; but an Englishman is never so happy as when he can prove that there is no real difference between black and white—and no more there is, in the dark. Our parlour Bolshevists are usually very young people, with an amiable sympathy with the under-dog, and a realisation that Puritanism, especially in its later phases, has been apt to forget the sternness of Christianity against acquisitiveness. So far they are right, and their hearts warm to the slogan: 'To each according to his needs; from each according to his ability'. But I will ask them to listen to what I shall have to say presently about the teaching of the Gospels.

Well—I have galloped through two thousand years of history. Are we any nearer to an answer to the question 'What is Christianity?'? It seems that we have a wide choice. Where shall we find our typical Christian? Origen the scholar, Blandina in the arena at Lyons, Simeon Stylites on his pillar, Gregory the Great, Thomas Aquinas, Thomas à Kempis, Ignatius of Loyola, Oliver Cromwell, George Fox and Woolman the Quakers, Howard the philanthropist, General Gordon? A strange collection indeed!

I must make my choice for the purpose of this paper, and this is my choice. I take as normative the Christ of the Synoptic Gospels. I will not discuss—and we can never know for certain—how far what we read about His life and teaching is representative or even always accurate. It may or may not be exactly what He taught—personally I think it is probably a very faithful record—but it is what the earliest Church learnt and assimilated, and we cannot go back any farther.

But we must make up our minds as to the character of our Lord's mission. I think the so-called 'eschatological' theory of Schweitzer—that Christ went about predicting a supernatural 'end of the age', a sudden catastrophe bringing the present world order to an end—that this was the basis of his teaching, and the rest only an 'Interim-Ethic' for the few months or years before the catastrophe—I think that this theory has now been almost abandoned. If we accept it, there is really nothing left of Christianity, for a prophet who went about telling people that the world was coming to an end when nothing of the sort was going to happen, would be a most mischievous person, unfit to be at large.

My view is that Christ came among His people as a prophet, that His message was religious and moral, in no way political; that He preached (like the old prophets) a lay religion, and paid for it with His life. I think further that the substance of

His teaching, though in some ways highly original, is very plain and unmistakable; that it transcends all local and temporal limits, and is both universal and individual.

I will be as brief as I can, but I must try and summarise what I believe to be essential in the message of the Gospels.

The foundation is a firm belief in a God with whom personal relations are possible—personal to a degree which we shall hardly find in Greek thought. He spoke of God as 'my Father', prayed to Him at all times, was convinced that He was sent by God to carry out His mission, and that in every detail of life He and all men are immediately under the eye and care of God.

From the Fatherhood of God follows the Brotherhood of man. We are a great family and should be united together in love. Christian love is no mere sentiment; it is the recognition of a fact involving a claim. In family life love, not justice, is the spring of action. Accordingly, in Christian ethics love holds the place which righteousness did for the Jews, and justice—'render to all their dues'—for the Greeks. The rule of thumb is 'do unto all men as ye would they should do unto you'. There is no difference of treatment towards friends and enemies (this is quite new).

He abolishes all man-made barriers by ignoring them. 'In Christ', as St Paul rightly explains, 'neither circumcision availeth anything, nor uncircumcision; but faith which worketh by love.' This again is new and immensely important, especially now.

Immediate access to God—no intermediaries. Temple and hierarchy abolished in principle. No attempt to organise a Church.

No harsh asceticism. He mixed freely in society and gave offence by doing so.

Rather tolerant of purely disreputable sins, and still more of ritual sins.

He hated three things—hypocrisy, hard-heartedness, and calculating worldliness.

He never holds out any hope of wide acceptance and popularity.

Fundamentally, all this rests on a quite definite standard of values, which are individual and universal. It contains no thought of social reform or political revolution.

There is no doubt what kind of life He thinks most favourable to spiritual well-being—it is that with which he was familiar. The Galileans were poor, not very poor, a well-educated and self-respecting peasantry, in a country where wants are easily satisfied. Anxiety about money He condemns with a quite new severity—it is all unnecessary. The acquisitive man is not 'thou thief', but 'thou fool'. The miser wastes his time and thought, which he should give to more important things. How can he 'enter into the Kingdom of Heaven' when his mind is choked with cares?

Thus He demonetises the world's currency. He despises all the paraphernalia of civilisation. 'A man's life consisteth not in the abundance of the things that he possesseth.'

Nothing can be further removed from the bitter preoccupation with economic questions which poisons modern politics. 'Seek ye first the kingdom of God, and his righteousness, and all these things shall be added unto you.' Get your values right, and you will be able to live happily together. In a world of claims and counterclaims there can be no peace.

Of course, He taught a future judgment and a future life. It is very difficult to tell what he really believed about these subjects. He accepted the current language and symbolism and did not dwell very much on them. The choice we all have to make is terribly important; He makes no attempt to soften what his contemporaries believed about hell, and about the devil. Nor does He soften the claim to 'forsake all and follow Him', even to the Cross. A very austere creed, a creed for heroes.

Matthew Arnold, as is well known, speaks of 'the secret and method of Jesus'. The word secret is not happily chosen;

he refers to the remarkable words 'whosoever will save his
life shall lose it'. We must not look in the Gospels for any
philosophical refinements about personality. What Christ
means is that we must be willing to give all to win all—like
the parable of the pearl of great price, and the fine lines of
Manilius: 'quid caelo dabimus? quantum est quo veneat
omne? impendendus homo est, deus esse ut possit in ipso.'
    The 'method' is 'cleanse the inside of the cup'. All reform
must be from within outwards, from the individual to society.
This is of immense and fundamental importance, as Carlyle
shows in a noble passage. We must choose between Christ
and Jean-Jacques Rousseau. The Communists themselves see
that this difference is crucial. We may quote a Latin author
again, Horace this time: 'sincerum est nisi vas, quodcumque
infundis acescit.' From within, out of the heart, comes all
that can ennoble and all that can defile us.
    These are the essential parts of Christ's Gospel as a rule of
life. But of course He belonged to His own time and country.
He was no legislator, even for Palestine in His own day; still
less did He ever think of leaving a code for societies living
in conditions which never came within His purview at all.
Just as we cannot imitate Christ by leading the life of a
wandering preacher and renouncing all social ties, so we
cannot build up a programme of Christian politics and
economics out of the Sermon on the Mount. We have to
apply broad principles to circumstances very unlike those
of Jewry under the Roman procurators and the Jerusalem
hierarchy.
    The Gospel, as I have said, is religious and moral, not
political. It aims at spiritual redemption, not at social reform.
And the first thing to insist upon is that the standard of values
is absolute, not dependent on any temporal, local, or political
circumstances. Love of God, love of neighbour, free and
open sincerity, sympathy with all who need it, freedom from
anxiety, a very light estimate of creature comforts, no sectional loyalties interfering with the flow of goodwill to all,

courage and self-sacrifice even to death, these are qualities which are the same always and everywhere. Against these, as always and everywhere wrong, are hatred, selfishness, greed, hard heartedness, calculating worldliness, hypocrisy, bitter party spirit in home or foreign politics, unscrupulousness, treachery, ingratitude—most of them based on materialism and acquisitiveness, which are quite independent of our station in life.

The character which I have summed up as that of a good Christian is not so very uncommon. We all know men and women like that. And if this character were universal, or very much commoner than it is, would not the world be a very pleasant place to live in, and would not most of our social evils simply disappear? I think they would.

Well then, this is the Christian contribution to social betterment. It is religious and moral. It does not inhibit legislative action or any other secular agencies for remedying human ills. If these are well conceived, the Christian will probably support them. But religion deals with individual character. Its message is 'get your values right'. 'Seek ye first the Kingdom of God, and his righteousness, and all these things shall be added unto you.' 'The Kingdom of God is not meat and drink, but righteousness and peace and joy in the Holy Ghost.' Peace and goodwill—simple enough! But good heavens, what a place the world would be if we believed in and practised them!

I have made my choice—what I mean by Christianity is the mind of Christ, and the standard of values which is quite clearly laid down in the Synoptic Gospels and the other parts of the New Testament.

But this is only half my task. For the Christianity which became a world religion was not merely the Palestinian Gospel, which like Buddhism failed to take root in the country of its origin. The Catholic Church is the heir of the Roman Empire, and belongs to Hellenistic civilisation. This means that it amalgamated with the religious philosophy of the time—Neoplatonism, a syncretistic system which owed most to Plato, but something to Aristotle and on the ethical side to the Stoa. Clement of Alexandria, Origen, the two Gregorys, and Augustine were all Platonists, and the Pseudo-Dionysius, a disciple of Proclus, had a great influence. Greek was almost lost in the West in the Dark Ages, but Erigena knew 'Dionysius' and his mystical philosophy. Eckhart was a modern Platonist. St Thomas Aquinas is mainly Aristotelian, but even he owed much to Platonism.

I am not forgetting the limits of my subject. But from St Paul downwards, Christianity has had an intellectual side which did not come from Palestine; it is and always must be more than an ethical system; it is also a religious philosophy.

When the Roman Catholics speak of the *philosophia perennis*, they mean the later Greek philosophy modified by what they hold to be divine revelation, and by the historical element which belongs to Palestine. Its chief exponent is still Aquinas.

I do not think any student of dogma and Christian theology can deny that our religion is not hospitable to all and every philosophical system. From St Paul downwards, it has been so bound up with Platonism that Plato can never be torn out of its side. This means that many philosophies, some of which are now influential, are definitely non-Christian, and I need not say that philosophy has a great deal to do with conduct.

Metaphysical dualism is excluded. Christianity has never solved the problem of evil, but it cannot accept the view that Ormuzd and Ahriman are contending on nearly equal terms in the arena.

Pantheism is excluded, though divine immanence is accepted. God is not equally present everywhere. Such a view is incompatible with the personality of God, and with His moral goodness. Greek thought never emphasised personality, and we may shrink from saying that God is 'a Person', but both dogma and experience are insistent that man may have personal relations with God: e.g. He knows and cares for us all, and can hear and answer prayer.

The world of common experience is only partly real. It partly reveals and partly conceals the real spiritual world, Plato's *cosmos noëtos* which is apprehended not by reasoning (*dianoia*) but by *nous*. Christian theology from St Paul prefers *pneuma* to *nous*, but the two are really the same.

This spiritual world, in which the three ultimate values, Goodness, Truth and Beauty, the content of the mind of God as knowable to man, are realised and operative, is no mere ideal but eternal fact. It is beyond Time and Space, but can be realised by us only under spatial and temporal forms. Hence Christian eschatology is symbolic, and, it must be owned, a mass of contradiction if we forget that 'eye hath not seen, nor ear heard, neither have entered into the heart of man, the things which God hath prepared for them that love Him'.

So far as we know, our lives here determine our status in eternity. The popular ideas that there will be a second paper for those near the borderline (the Protestant and quite erroneous conception of Purgatory); that there will be any kind of future probation; that all will be saved at the last, are no part of the Christian religion, though we may believe them if we choose.

The notions that there is 'one increasing purpose' (whatever that means) in the time-process; that there is one far off divine event; that either the universe or part of it is progressing towards perfection; that God is in any way involved in this process, so that we may say that He is realising Himself in the world, that the world is as necessary to Him as He is to the world, that He ever will be what He is not—all these ideas belong to the modern delusion of a law of progress in Time; they are not only not Christian, but are incompatible with Christian theism. The same applies to the divinisation of Time in writers like Bergson and Croce.

The ultimate values are essentially creative in the phenomenal world. For us, there is no contemplation without action. 'See that thou make all things according to the pattern shown thee in the mount.'

The question how happenings in time can affect the eternal world cannot be answered by Christian philosophy. Like the problem of evil, it is a ragged edge, an insoluble problem.

In the individual life, progress in grace and knowledge of reality proceed *pari passu*. We only see what is like ourselves; we surround ourselves with a world after our own likeness. The first stage is Faith—the resolution to stand or fall by the noblest hypothesis; then Faith justifies itself as Knowledge; and Knowledge (so says Clement of Alexandria), as it passes into Love, unifies the Knower and the Known, and makes man 'equal to the angels'. This in a nutshell is the scheme and theory of Christian morality, which is a reasoned philosophy based on inner experience, not a mere *Schwärmerei* or emotional state.

These ultimate beliefs must deeply affect our opinions as to the social, educational, and international relevance of Christianity. For our religion is not mere humanism. Humanism is not far from the Kingdom of God, but its standard of values is a rather muddled utilitarianism; its idealism is mainly sentimental and emotional. We need definite conviction about ultimate reality.

I fully admit that our standards of right and wrong differ widely in certain respects from what the Catholic Church has usually taught, and that modern humanism has been of great value. For instance, our duty to posterity could not be emphasised when it was believed that 'the Judge is at the gate'. Cruelty, for some inexplicable reason, was not reckoned among the deadly sins. We do not now think that adultery and apostasy should be ranked with murder as offences for which 'even Christ will not ask that we may be pardoned'. We do not now think that since animals have no souls, they have no rights. We certainly do not think that all who do not belong to our branch of the Church will be damned. But you will remember that I answered the question, 'What is Christianity?' by 'the teaching of Christ', not by the traditions of the Church. On the whole, I think that in ethics we have come back nearer to the original Gospel. But we must beware of being carried away by the slogans of the day, which often echo the science and philosophy of the day before yesterday; by the callow exuberance of youth, which thinks of putting the world to rights when it ought to be thinking of passing its examinations; by the pontifical rhetoric of armchair revolutionists; and by the sinister activities of crooked and ambitious politicians. After all, there never has been a time when the common man was as well off as he is now. We are at last a civilised nation, instead of a nation with a civilised class. Equality of opportunity may be extended still further; but surely bitter and excited language is out of place. A church never goes into politics without coming out badly smirched. Its answer to its critics should be, 'Who made me a judge or a divider over you? Take heed and beware of all covetousness, for a man's life consisteth not in the abundance of the things that he possesseth.' The alternative, I am afraid, is a war of extermination, with the unexampled horrors which we have witnessed in Russia and Spain. For the saying of Anatole France is true. If you begin by thinking that human nature is innocent, and only institutions evil, you will end by wishing to murder all who do not agree with you.

I need not say much, even if I had time, on the unspeakable abomination of war. It is just because it has lost its veneer of chivalry, and become morally damnable, that those who engage in it set no limits to their wickedness. There never has been a time till our own when belligerents would stick at nothing. I do not understand this diabolism. What Christ would have thought of it needs no argument or explanation.

THE CHRISTIAN MOVEMENT IN EDUCATION

John Macmurray

NOTHING would afford me greater pleasure than to give a simple, practical address on this subject which might help the educationist to find a way of making religion an effective element in the teaching of the young. On all sides I find an increasing awareness of the importance of religion in the field of education, coupled with a feeling of impotence when it comes to determining how religion can be effectively taught. I should like to be able to give some practical and immediate help. Yet I find that I cannot. Convinced as I am that religion is the element in human life which is of the utmost importance; and that education is either a religious task or it is not true education, I am unable to say anything on the subject which has an immediate practical bearing. For if I tried to do so—as I have tried before—I should be misunderstood, and my advice, if it were taken, would lead to efforts which would be useless, if not positively harmful.

I am thrown back on an effort to explain why this is so; to explain why it is that we are unable to do what we feel to be of such importance, or even to understand what it is that we are failing to do. If we can get this clear, then at least we shall be able to state the practical problem rightly. And that itself will take us a considerable way in the direction of a solution.

The root of the difficulty lies in the fact that we Europeans are not religious; and our cultural heritage is not a religious one. We have a religion. Indeed, we have quite a number of religions. That only proves that we are not religious. A religious man does not 'have' a religion, any more than a scientific man 'has' a science. Religion is not a particular and separate department of life. It is a way of knowing life and living it. It is a way of apprehending the world and our existence in it, rather than something in the world that we apprehend. It is not something that we think about, but a way of thinking anything and everything. It is a mode of consciousness, and the only mode of consciousness that is adequate to focus and enfold the whole of our human experience. Our trouble is that when we think religion we think it in a non-religious mode of consciousness, and so completely fail to understand it.

We have to begin by recognising that there are different modes of consciousness; and that the same statements, if apprehended in different modes of consciousness, have quite different meanings. This is an unfamiliar notion, and it is not an easy one to grasp. The simplest way to recognise the difference between modes of consciousness is to begin by recalling the kinds of experience in which it makes itself felt. Most of you must have had the experience of discussing some complex topic with persons of another nationality. If you have, you will know how difficult it is to understand their meaning or to make them understand yours. In such discussions we are continually finding ourselves talking at cross-purposes. Normally, we account for this by the fact that one or other of us is talking in a foreign language. But this is not always so. I myself find it more difficult, in some ways, to carry on a discussion with an American than with a German. We speak the same language. We use the same words and phrases. We take it for granted that we mean the same things by them. Sooner or later we discover that this is not so. The overtones, the associations, the references of words and phrases are different. In the result we fail, at critical points, to understand one another.

In this case the difference is not very wide. It is merely a difference in the social context in which the language has been learned and used. Let us take other instances. When we read the works of men of older civilisations than our own,

we tend to assume that they must have meant what we ourselves would mean if we used the same words and phrases.
A moment's reflection will show that, where the meaning of
the ideas we are expressing has been modified in the centuries
which have passed since their books were written, this assumption must be false. When we think of Galileo's dropping
two unequal weights from the leaning tower of Pisa—
whether he ever did perform the experiment or not is of no
consequence—the fact that they reached the ground together
is for us conclusive proof that bodies do not fall to the ground
with a velocity proportional to their weight. It is difficult
for us to recognise that to the devout conservatism of the
time it proved conclusively that Galileo was in league with
the Devil. It is difficult for an English lecturer on political
theory to abstain from quoting with relish and approval
Aristotle's assertion that 'Man is a social animal.' Yet there
is something ludicrous in this appeal to the ancient authority.
For the background of the philosopher's phrase is well
expressed in the words of Pericles' funeral oration at the end
of the first year of the Peloponnesian war, when he boasted
that the Athenians abhorred the ἴδιος—the man who lived
a private life of his own. We might paraphrase Aristotle's
dictum flippantly by saying 'Man is a creature who likes to
get out of his house in the morning to tell the first stranger he
meets about the quarrel he had with his wife over breakfast.'
No English lecturer could mean that.

These instances may serve to indicate the kind of difficulty
in understanding words and phrases that I have in mind,
when I say that the meaning of statements may depend on
the mode of consciousness in which they are apprehended.
Meaning varies with its mental context; with the overtones,
associations, and references of the words and phrases which
convey it. Many of these variations depend on simple
differences of environment and empirical experience. But
some of them depend on fundamental attitudes of mind
which condition our experience. It is to these that I refer

when I speak of 'modes of consciousness'. There are three which must be distinguished—the personal, the contemplative, and the practical. In terms of their reflective expressions in culture they may be called the religious mode, the aesthetic mode, and the scientific mode. In these three modes the same statements have quite different meanings, because they have different references and associations. A statement made in the religious mode must be totally misunderstood if it is heard in the scientific or the aesthetic mode.

Now there are three cultural traditions which have gone to the making of our own—the Hebrew, the Greek, and the Roman. The Hebrew tradition is in the religious mode, the Greek is in the aesthetic mode, and the Roman in the scientific. Of these three traditions the Hebrew tradition has never been consciously assimilated by Europe. It works as a ferment in the Unconscious, like leaven in the meal. We can neither escape from Christianity, nor can we accept it. Our consciousness is not religious; yet the impact of the Hebrew religious consciousness upon Europe makes it impossible for us to rest in either the aesthetic or the scientific mode, which alone are available. The restless, revolutionary, progressive character of European history is the consequence of this. Its driving force is Christianity—but a Christianity that we are not capable of thinking or intending. In our conscious life we are dualists, swinging from an aesthetic to a scientific consciousness of the world, neither of which feels adequate, and neither of which can release us into action. For the two modes inhibit one another. We tumble about between an aesthetic idealism and a utilitarian realism, and in both remain in the field of theory. Consequently, our religion is not merely theoretical, it is also unthinkable. For to think it we have only the choice between an aesthetic and a scientific mode of consciousness, neither of which is adequate to its reality. And the more our civilisation comes to depend on conscious understanding, the more evident and disastrous grows our inability to conceive and intend Christianity.

Consider some of the symptoms of this malady for a a moment. Our religion is bound up with the supernatural. We can only think it as above and beyond the world in which we live, as a shadowy reduplication of our real life. We have to *turn* to religion, away from the world. We are conscious of a gulf fixed between our secular and our religious life. In order to live in this world we have to turn from religion. We cannot carry our religious experience across the gulf into our ordinary life. Our theology, as the conscious expression of our religious beliefs, draws its intellectual forms entirely from Greek philosophy; from Stoicism; from neo-Platonism; from Aristotelianism; all of them forms of thought untouched by Christian influence. We contrast it with the naturalism and empiricism of modern scientific thought, which within its limits is profoundly influenced by Christianity. Quite early European religious organisations divided into a Western and an Eastern form; the one Greek, aesthetic and mystical in nature; the other Roman, practical and legal. And both of them ran parallel to the corresponding secular life instead of penetrating and informing it. All these dualisms bear witness to our incapacity to think the natural world religiously or even to comprehend the possibility of doing so.

The effect of the dualism upon our understanding of the natural world is very great. Whatever in the natural course of events we associate with religion has to be excluded from the world and thought in separation from it.

If we think of God acting in the ordinary world, then we must think a miracle—an interference with the course of nature, which must be inexplicable. This merely means that we cannot think any causal relation between our religious and our secular experience. And this involves extruding from our secular conception of history everything that is reckoned as 'religious'. Our historians, therefore, have to explain the history of European thought without referring to Christianity or Christian theology. They must understand the development of modern society as if Jesus and Paul had no part in it, since they 'belong to the religious world'. Since the ancient Hebrews and their influence upon the world are 'religious' subjects, history must pass them by as non-existent for scientific purposes. A great classical scholar can assert that whatever moves in the modern world was started by the Greeks; and no one, not even religious people, will notice how grotesque the statement is. The same people, in a religious mood, will point to the progress and advance of civilisation in European history as clear evidence of the gradual fulfilment of the mission of Christ for the salvation of the world, and the glaring contradiction will never appear. Why not? Because there are two minds in us which do not come into contact. Because we do not and cannot think the two things at once. We can sincerely assert our belief in miracles in church or in 'religious' discussion, but we cannot believe in miracles happening in the world which contains the Stock Exchange, scientific inventions, and rearmament.

So when we waken up to the fact that the breakdown of religion is having a demoralising effect upon our secular life, and that education ought to be doing something to stop the rot, we are in a quandary. We demand religious education. We seek to teach religion in our schools. What happens? We find a place in our curriculum for religion as a 'subject', as one subject amongst others. What does this subject consist of? 'Religious' literature, 'religious' history, 'religious' philosophy, metaphysical and ethical. But we already have classes in history and literature and philosophy. Why do we need to reduplicate these subjects? Because there is a part of 'history' that is not really history, a part of 'literature' that is not really literature, and so on. In other words, the methods and criteria which we employ and demand in the understanding of history or the appreciation of literature do not apply to 'religious' history or to 'religious' literature. The effect will be to teach our pupils that religion is fantasy; that it has no connection with real life; that it belongs to a world where all questions about what is true and what is false, what is beautiful and what is ugly are, and must be, kept in abeyance. During the 'religious' period what would be incredible in every other has to be believed; and all critical doubts and all demands for proof which are insisted upon in other fields must be silenced. Surely this is not religious education, but education for the dissociation of religion from real life. And its result—so far as it is success-ful—must be practical atheism. Until we can teach religious history in the history class and religious literature in the literature class without a sense of incongruity; until we can think religious beliefs in the same mode of consciousness in which we think secular beliefs, it is useless to attempt to bring religion into the curriculum at all.

What, then, are the characteristics of the religious con-sciousness? I think that the best answer is a reference to the Jews, particularly to the old Hebrew culture of which the Old and New Testaments are the product and the expression. But this reference is not to the content of the Bible primarily, but to the mode of consciousness which it expresses. We have to think of the difference in mental atmosphere which we find when we turn from the Greek philosophers to the Hebrew prophets, or from the Roman to the Jewish con-ception of law and social organisation. Above all we have to notice the absence of dualism in Hebrew consciousness. The Jewish community which the Old Testament reveals is a religious community, groping its way through history to a satisfactory religious view of the world and of the life of the community in it. The New Testament is its final outcome, in which it found (and rejected) what it had been seeking. The New Testament is as much a Jewish book as the Old. Christianity, it must always be remembered, is essentially Jewish. This Jewish community does not 'have' a religion. It is not trying to graft a religious belief on to the secularism of its social life. The reflection of the prophets, by which religion develops and comes to a fuller understanding, is not 'philosophical' or idealist. It is a constant reflection upon actual history. The Hebrew historian thinks history in terms of God. We cannot think history like that. Where we say 'Nelson won the battle of Trafalgar', the Jew says, 'The Lord brought his people up out of the land of Egypt.' And because his secular history is thought religiously, no dualism between religion and politics, or between law and morality arises. It is not necessary to turn to another world to find the substance of religious experience. There is no room and no need for mysticism or idealism. Religious statements are about common fact.

This difference between our own mode of consciousness and the Hebrew mode is strikingly evident in the contemporary struggle for and against religion. It is a struggle for or against a belief in the supernatural. The anti-religious forces wish to concentrate our hopes, aspirations and efforts upon this world. They attack otherworldliness and idealism and the hope of immortality because these divert our energies from the task of creating heaven upon earth. If men are to devote their energies and enthusiasm and creativeness to the salvation of the world, they feel they must stop believing in God and get rid of religion altogether. Underlying this conviction lies the assumption that religion consists essentially of the belief in immortality and another world than this. The defenders of religion accept this assumption. The belief in another world and another life is to them also the essence of religion. Both sides have something in common—a conception of religion as referring to something other than our life in this world. Both agree that to destroy the belief in immortality and the other world would mean *ipso facto* the disappearance of religion. Yet this conception of religion is demonstrably false. For if it were true, it would imply that the ancient Hebrews, whose classical literature the Old Testament is, were unique among the peoples of the world in being totally non-religious. Could anything be more absurd? It is true that the ancient Hebrews did not develop a belief in immortality. There is no evidence of it in the Old Testament; neither is there any otherworldliness. Yet the uniqueness of the Hebrews lies in the fact that they produced the only religious civilisation that the world has yet seen.

At this point again we must be on our guard against misunderstanding. We are discussing the form of religious consciousness, not the particular beliefs which it produces at any particular period of its development. It is not the truth of a religious belief that makes it religious any more than it is the truth of a scientific belief that makes it scientific. That the ancient Hebrews had no doctrine of immortality does not disprove immortality. What it does prove is that there is nothing in the character of religious consciousness which inevitably compels it to refer to another life and another world. It can think this life and this world religiously without the sense that something is left out. The scientific mode of consciousness cannot do this. Neither can the aesthetic. Both compel us into dualism and idealism because they provide us with views of the world which leave out something that we know is there. So we have to construct an imaginary world to contain what they leave out. For the religious consciousness, however, God is not supernatural but perfectly natural.

What is it that is left out by other modes of consciousness and included in the religious mode? It is simply the personal element in our experience. What we cannot conceive is a personal world; and a personal world is a world that can contain persons and their personal lives and their personal relationships. The scientific consciousness excludes anthropomorphism. This may be all very well when we are trying to understand Matter or Life. We have then to overcome the tendency to think of the behaviour of rocks or cabbages as if it were the behaviour of people. But what will happen to the scientific consciousness when it tries to conceive and understand the behaviour of human beings? Its impersonality, its exclusion of anthropomorphism, will simply mean that it must treat human beings as if they were not human beings. And where the scientific consciousness is made the basis of human relationship it will merely mean that we behave to one another as if we were not human beings—inhumanly. Thought that can be the basis of an intentional construction of human life, of human society—which can understand and direct human life for human purposes, must necessarily be religious. It must be capable of thinking the world in human terms, which means in terms of God. Humanism rests on the belief that human beings are animals and not human at all; because thought depends on universals, and therefore particular instances of personality can only be thought in terms of universal personality. The denial of God is man's self-negation, since it is the denial of personality. And it is absurd; because we *are* persons, and our denial of personality is merely a perverse expression of what we deny.

I have said enough, I hope, to explain my difficulty in offering practical advice about religious teaching. How can we reasonably ask how to teach religion when we are so far from knowing what religion is? We have to rediscover it. In proportion as we do, the educational question will answer itself. To teach religion is to teach people to think the world— and therefore to think science, history, art, and every other subject—in terms of God. What we usually call religious instruction is largely teaching people to pretend that they believe in the unnatural. To call it the supernatural makes no difference. So far as we succeed we shall merely have taught them to live, in an imaginary world, another life than the one they must live in the world around them. And we shall have taught them to think and live their real lives in a world that has no place for God, and in a manner that stultifies their own humanity.

JUDAISM AND CHRISTIANITY

J. W. Parkes

TWENTY-FIVE years ago we used at intervals to have in our curriculum two periods—'Scripture (O.T.)', and 'Scripture (N.T.)'. These were periods when we comported ourselves like the gentleman in Aristophanes' *Acharnians* for three-quarters of an hour, while our clerical headmaster disported himself with his cat, hedgehog or parrot, or simply slumbered under a large bandanna handkerchief in an adjoining conservatory. As I do not know whether that is the method by which 'Scripture (O.T.)' and 'Scripture (N.T.)' are still taught, my remarks cannot take the form of criticism of existing methods, nor could they usefully do so, since I am signally ignorant of both boys and teaching. I can therefore only put forward a point of view on the relations of Judaism and Christianity. I do not know whether what I have to say, if right, is teachable, or how it is to be taught. That I must leave to others.

For the British Israelites the value of 'Scripture (O.T.)' consists in its being the history of their Jewish ancestors. For the fundamentalist it is the exposition of the Word of God. For the rest of us its value consists in its unique place in the story of God's dealing with man, of the same stuff as the story of Greece, Rome, or our own history, but claiming a special place in our thoughts, for its own transcendent fascination. Properly understood it illumines the history of the rest of us, and no other history can take its place. It is the story of how man found God, and how God revealed Himself to man, and as such it provides the keystone to the arch of history, not taking the place of any other stone in that arch, or essentially different from any other stone, but yet essential if the arch is to hold in place. In it the two ideas, to-day much frowned on, of progress and purpose are evident, and these two ideas unite Jewish history with that of the rest of the world, and do not divide it from them.

Palestine lies at the meeting-place of the cultures of the ancient world. Egypt, the Mediterranean, and Mesopotamia lay around it, and the highway from one to the other, by land, lay through its borders. And behind it lay the desert with its infinity. Out of this combination of circumstances there was born the union of the idea of God with the ideas of morals and ethics. All were present at the birth. But the child grew in Palestine among the Jews. There is a charming rabbinic legend which embodies this idea. Why was the Law given outside the borders of the country, in the desert? Because it was given equally to all people; but the Jews listened to it and accepted it. By slow, very slow stages the child grew. Among the many Gods it worshipped, it came to realise that this God who gave it a moral code was the most important; gradually it saw that this was, indeed, the only God for *it* to worship, while still accepting that there were other Gods, inferior to its own, who were worshipped by the peoples. It treated its God as did others, blustered with Him, threatened Him, cajoled Him, deceived Him, and, at times, ran away from Him, but gradually it sensed an incongruity in so behaving to One who was the source of its life and the Norm of its conduct. As Samuel, the child learnt that God demanded obedience; as Elijah, that He had a purpose and a power independent of the success or failure of His votaries. In these ways the child grew to adolescence, and the ground was slowly prepared for the second great step in the evolution of man's understanding of God, of God's revelation to man.

Browning describes how 'out of three sounds' the musician could make 'not a fourth sound, but a star', but the three sounds were the product of long preparation, and only when they were fully understood and mastered was there any element of suddenness—the sudden realisation that in these three familiar sounds in his ears he possessed a star. So the child, now a youth, putting together a God the source of moral standards of conduct, a God the only one for him to worship, a God independent of the success or failure of His worshippers, suddenly realised as Amos that this was the ONLY GOD THERE WAS, THE CREATOR AND SUSTAINER OF THE UNIVERSE. Monotheism was born, and its terrific implications crowded one upon another into the consciousness of the youth. It is difficult for us to realise the colossal shock which Amos must have caused to his religious contemporaries. His first appearance was at a national review; the Archbishop of the day had just pronounced an inspiring address to the forces about to depart to battle, when an ignorant countryman got up and started ranting about righteousness. We made it clear last Armistice day how much more adequately we could deal with such a situation. The less efficient police of Jeroboam II were nonplussed, and the countryman got away with it. It is very important to note that it is on Amos' basis of no favouritism, and of the greater responsibility of greater knowledge, that the doctrine of the Chosen People was developed.

After Amos, Hosea; after Hosea, Isaiah; after Isaiah, Jeremiah. With all the anonymous writings of the period of which scraps have survived, the period from the appearance of Amos to the fall of Jerusalem is one of the most brilliant in the history of mankind. The nature of God, the nature of man, their relations, the concept of human society, one idea after another received thrilling illumination, and literary expression of immortal beauty. The universalism and the conception of righteousness embodied in the prophetic utterances were embodied in new and richer codes of law; Amos and Isaiah were turned into Deuteronomy.

Even the Exile wrought no diminution of the stream of religious discovery and interpretation. The Holiness of God, the need of righteousness in man, and the universalism of God's interests were magnificently expressed in prophets, in law-books, and in scattered writings; and out of its bitterness was born in the great poet known as the Second Isaiah the first understanding of redemptive service through suffering.

Now the whole of this period had a characteristic which is too often overlooked. The new discoveries in the field of religion proceeded at such a rate that they left the ordinary man miles behind. The prophets had but few followers. The mass of the population from the throne to the peasant alternated between admiration, alarm, and indignation. They continued their old lip-service to Jahwe, and their cosy domestic arrangements with the many other deities whose temples were to be found in Jerusalem up to the last days of its independence.

There followed a period, no less brilliant, but much more often misunderstood. To consider that the main details of the religious story of Israel were completed when the last of the great prophets laid down his pen is the same as to consider that the religious history of England has no further interest after the last wandering missionary settled down into being a parish priest with a little church of his own and a little flock to teach. The truth was all there in the prophets, but it had missed the common people: it was impressive, but it did not apply to daily life. There arose then a class of teachers and law-makers, codifiers, and translators, most of whom were anonymous, who painstakingly, prosaically, and conscientiously turned the extravagances and visions of the prophets into the stuff of everyday life. It was they, not the prophets, who made monotheism the religion of the people; it was they who destroyed the last remnants of idolatry, who turned the universalism and the call for righteousness into rules of daily conduct, the unknown rabbis and scribes of early Judaism. To do this they introduced into the history of humanity ideas as striking as, though less dramatic than, those of their predecessors. To them we owe the idea of religious discipline; of religious education; of regular services of prayer, teaching, and worship; of the idea that religion as we know it was the inheritance of every man, not of a selected group.

We owe also to them, though they themselves hardly realised what they were contributing, the idea of progressive revelation—the essential foundation of intellectual sincerity in successive generations turning to the same written word as the foundation of their faith. It arose out of controversies between those groups whom we know later as the Sadducees and the Pharisees. The former insisted that the law of God covered precisely those points with which the written law dealt, and that they were free on all other matters to make laws for themselves. To this the Pharisees replied that the law of God must cover all of life; nothing could be outside of it. The written word was but the focus point through which God's infinite wisdom answered man's infinite needs, and *every generation had the duty of making its own interpretation for its own needs.* In this way they blended tradition with innovation in a way which has never been excelled.

Great as was their work, it suffered from an obvious danger. By its very contrast with the free and flowing utterance of the prophets, it ran the danger, and often fell into it, of becoming too meticulous, too precise, too prosaic. It made religion ecclesiastical and institutional, both necessary elements in religion, but dangerous ones. This precision and, one might say, pedestrianism was emphasised by a temporary phenomenon in Judaism, which yet left permanent effects. The conception of God left by the prophets, in its holiness and perfection made God Himself remote and unapproachable. In theology, in the strictest interpretation of that word, there was little advance, little further definition—in extraordinary contrast to the flood of theological speculation which accompanied the early centuries of the Church. It is almost true to say that with Ezekiel God passed beyond human understanding and comprehension, so that only by ritual acts could man approach Him; man's best moral efforts were so worthless compared to God's perfection that they meant nothing to Him. It would be a gross mistake to imply that in historical Judaism God is felt to be remote, but it remains true that Judaism retains a curiously undeveloped theology for a religion which has so stressed intellectual understanding.

It is, however, the merits of this period which seem to me to be infinitely more important than its defects, for it was these teachers who prepared and made possible the Incarnation which is the crown of their work. This is a phrase which is continuously misused, for the average Christian places the crown on a head which he is careful to state is a corpse, in exactly the same way as the preacher loves to call Jesus the fulfilment of the Law, and then to go on to say that the Law has ceased to exist. It appears to me to be difficult to fulfil that which has ceased to exist. I do not think that we can really understand the Incarnation except as the culmination of a continuous process which was not meant to be interrupted. Jesus came to say nothing new. Everything which He taught was already embodied in Pharisaic teaching. He came as the confirmation of the prophetic vision embodied in the highest Pharisaic ideal. His originality was His Person and His emphasis, in that He recalled men to the simple heart of things which was in danger of being lost in attention to conduct, and to the nearness of God which was in danger of being obscured in the majesty of His Holiness.

The Incarnation concludes the first stage in the history which we have been discussing, the story of man's discovery of God, and of God's revelation to man. It appears to me a total falsification of perspective to stop the 'O.T.' at Malachi, and begin the 'N.T.' with the life of Christ. His life belongs to the previous period. The *new* stage in the history of God's way with man begins with the attempt of his followers to understand what the life of Christ had meant, what His purpose had been, and what they were to do about it. It is a stage which opens with small beginnings, as had all previous stages in the world's evolution. Nothing seems to me to be farther from the truth than the idea that a triumphant Church, fully conscious of its mission and divinely instructed as to its purpose and organisation, began operations immediately after Pentecost, and that, since then, there has been a steady decline in Christian experience and understanding.

The truth is very different; the apostles were bewildered by the experience which had befallen them, and only slowly and tentatively began to find explanations for it. It was not for a generation that they thought of writing down their memories of the life and teaching of their Master, and it was a century before the Church began to take a shape recognisable as the ancestor of the institutions and doctrines of to-day.

It is during this intermediate period that the decisive steps were unhappily taken in the relation of those Jews who had come to believe that in Jesus of Nazareth had appeared the Messiah, to those who did not. By the beginning of the second century Christianity and Judaism were recognisable, even to the Roman authorities, as two separate religions. The stages of that separation, as they are revealed in and through the New Testament, are of enormous significance.

In so far as the life of Christ is concerned, it is of great importance to recognise that all the Gospels were written during the different phases of the controversy, and all are coloured, consciously or unconsciously, by the attitude of the author to it. One or two examples will illustrate the change which was taking place during the period. Mark, in describing the healing of the man with palsy (ii. 1 ff.), makes Jesus ask the neutral question of the scribes: 'Why reason ye these things in your hearts.' In Matthew the question is so turned that it is presumed that the attitude of the scribes is hostile: 'Why think ye evil in your hearts' (ix. 1 ff.), and all the story contains a heightened colouring. In Mark the relations between Jesus and the Pharisees open in a normal fashion, and the opposition between them is developed in an understandable way. In Luke the people of Nazareth try to kill Him almost at the beginning of His ministry. In John there is deadly enmity from the very first, and Jesus calls even those Jews which had believed on Him children of their father the Devil. The Synoptic Gospels know nothing of any responsibility of the Pharisees for the arrest, trial, and death of Jesus; in John (xii. 42), at the end, many of the rulers are said to believe in Him, but to be afraid to confess it for fear of the Pharisees.

The actual development of the relations of Jesus to Jewish parties of His day appears to have been as follows. There was nothing unorthodox in the beginning of His preaching. He drew large crowds; and, naturally, the local religious leaders, who would have been Pharisees, heard of and wished to examine this new youthful preacher. On various occasions they questioned Him. His replies gradually revealed a liberalism which they considered to be dangerous. The local Pharisees got the advice of their leaders in Jerusalem. They studied Him and advised the crowd to leave Him alone. His teaching was too broad. His indifference to matters which seemed to them important was dangerous. There was no question of His being schismatic or setting Himself up as a scribe against them; His attitude on that score was correct; but He was a latitudinarian and a modernist, and the times were too dangerous to permit of such. In spite of the condemnation of the Pharisees, His influence grew. The political authorities, alarmed for their security, also took an interest in Him and quickly decided that He was better out of the way. A judicial murder was arranged, and they considered that the incident was closed. Throughout there was no question of Jesus founding a separate church; that He had gathered disciples only meant that He had done what every Jewish teacher did. No act or word of His was incompatible with Judaism, even though His conduct and ideas were sometimes lax from the standard of strict Pharisaism.

The apostles certainly thought of themselves as Jews, Jews who knew the name of the Messiah, but orthodox Jews of different colours, James a Pharisee, some laxer, some more

nationalist, and so on. They spent much of their time in the
Temple, and it is frequently said that, but for the genius of
Paul, Christianity would have remained an unimportant
Jewish sect at Jerusalem. This omits an essential feature of the
situation. These Jews believed that they were living in the
Messianic age, and every Jew knew that when Messiah came
a new relationship with the Gentiles would be created, for
the kingdom of Messiah was universal. If some thought of
this relationship in terms of conquest, the Pharisees and others
thought of it in terms of religious conversion. Paul neither
created nor determined the lines of the admission of the
Gentiles. That was done by the orthodox Jewish Church in
Jerusalem.

The first adherents, however, were men with some knowledge of Judaism and Jewish ceremonial; the new feature of
Paul's mission was his conversion of pure pagans. This posed,
at once, the problem of the ceremonial law. In spite of all
modern critics, I still think that the description of the council
of Jerusalem in Acts xv is substantially accurate. Paul submitted the question to Jerusalem. A thoroughly sensible
solution was decided on (I believe Luke's account of the
decisions embodies the Noachic Commandments, and are
not food laws), and Paul and the Jerusalem Church continued
in complete harmony with their respective tasks.

One party in the Church disagreed—the people known as
the Judaisers who are not to be confused with the Church of
Jerusalem, the Judeo-Christians. To-day, we should call them
'spikes'. Some of them strict Pharisees, some of them probably converts, for converts are often 'plus catholiques que le
Pape'. They wished to insist on the strict observance of the
ceremonial law. Against their teaching, which began before
the council met, Paul, on his way probably to Jerusalem,
hurled the violent diatribes of the Epistle to the Galatians.
The council confirmed his point of view, and for the rest of
his missionary life Paul continued with the curious dualism,
which is typical of young movements, but which obviously

could not have survived for long without modification—the moral and ceremonial law for Jewish believers in the Messiah, the moral law only for Gentiles. This dualism, and the fact that Paul's contemporaries knew when he was talking about the ceremonial law and when he was not, explain the apparent contradictions between Acts and the Epistles.

As to Paul himself, I do not believe that he ever dreamed that he had ceased to be an orthodox Pharisaic Jew in accepting Jesus as his Messiah. The conception of Paul breaking with Judaism as the essential basis of the growth of the Church is totally inaccurate. His morals were strictly Jewish; he observed the feasts at Jerusalem and would even break off a missionary journey to observe them; allowing for his habit of letting his pen run away with him when deeply moved (witness his contrite remarks to the Corinthians on the subject) there is not a word which he wrote inconsistent with the beliefs of a Pharisee who held that he was living in the Messianic age and who wanted to explain his Jewish Messiah to Gentiles in the language which they would most easily understand. It is this which explains so much of the phraseology of the mystery religions in his letters; words of great value to his purpose, but devastating in their effects on subsequent Christian theology. His message has nothing to do with salvation in a future life, of predestination, but with power in Christ. It is doubtful if Paul would have understood a word of the doctrines Augustine built upon his foundation, and his language about the Judaisers would have been laudatory compared to his comments on Calvin or Barth as exponents of his gospel.

Paul undoubtedly caused violent controversy within the Jewish communities, but not more than the situation warranted, or more than the Jews were accustomed to. What made a separation inevitable was the misinterpretations of Paul's remarks about the Law by followers and successors who did not know the meaning of the word. This is not to say that those Jews who did not accept Paul's view that Jesus was the Messiah were behaving in angelic fashion, and that the whole responsibility for the schism lay on one side. The early believers in Jesus, Jew and Gentile, suffered a good deal from the officials and public of the Synagogues, and their stories of the wonderful life of Jesus were countered by others showing him in an unfavourable light. But if the ultimate statement of the Synagogue that no man can accept Jesus as Messiah and remain a member was a tragic error, so was the statement of the Christians that no man who accepts Jesus as Messiah may observe the Law.

On both sides the unhappy results of that separation are still with us. With what the Jews have lost I am not here concerned, but with the losses of the Gentile Church. If it has kept the person of Jesus, it has surrendered a very large part of His religion, parts which the Synagogue has retained. The exaggerated emphasis on the next world, on emotion as opposed to understanding, on the heart as opposed to the head, on the individual as opposed to the community, these together with many superstitions taken over from the pagan world, historic Christianity owes to her break with the Synagogue, and if we reflect on the needs of religion to-day, and on the various weak points in its armour as it confronts the modern world, it is astonishing how many of these rise out of the tragedy of the beginning of the second century eighteen hundred years ago.

PART II

DEVELOPMENTS IN ORGANISATION AND CURRICULUM IN PUBLIC SCHOOLS

F. R. G. Duckworth

As you probably know, most of the public schools have submitted themselves of their own free will to inspection at the hands of the Board of Education. Some of them in the last twenty years or so have been inspected as many as three times. So it occurred to me, when I was invited to address you at this Conference, that by carefully reading the reports on those inspections one might get, as it were, a documented account of the changes and developments in public schools since about 1910 which would not be without its interest. And perhaps indeed that task might be carried out with advantage by some one with a greater amount of time than was at my disposal. Actually, I found myself forced to confine the scope of my enquiries within somewhat narrow limits which are sufficiently indicated by the title of this address.

One thing is certain—and it did not need a laborious scrutiny of staid departmental documents to establish this— that the changes which have taken place during the last thirty years in the education given in public schools have been fundamental and have been rapidly made. And this development broadly viewed is part of a movement of remarkable force, a veritable renaissance, which has been and still is remoulding all forms of education in this country. The beginnings of the movement, so far as it has directly affected public schools, can be traced back to the influence of a line of great headmasters—Thomas Arnold, Edward Thring, Frederick William Sanderson and, in our own day, Cyril Norwood, whom it will not be invidious to mention within these precincts. Nor must one forget, outside the ranks of schoolmasters, Matthew Arnold, that singular man who contrived to be at once an inspector of schools and a poet. Legislation arising out of this movement of ideas and taking shape in the Education Act of 1902 was destined, by creating a system of state-aided secondary education, powerfully though indirectly to exercise influence on the education given in public schools. I note two other manifestations of the forces at work. The first is the growth of interest in professional training for teachers. The traditional belief of the public school master that teaching is a matter of divine afflatus helped out by much bellowing and cursing, is pretty well dead now or survives only in the antics of Mr Will Hay. The second force was the growing influence of psychology as applied to education and the changes which have been wrought in the doctrine and methods of psychology itself. From the point of view of my subject this morning one such change is particularly important—I mean the exploding of what is known as the faculty psychology with its attendant theory of mental discipline—the theory that, for example, Latin Prose develops the faculties of lucidity and precision.

So much by way of attempting to find a setting for the topic. It will be in order, now, to attempt a rough sketch of the curriculum and organisation of work in public schools at the opening of the present century. Classics still held the pride of place, although modern sides had been introduced partly on educational grounds, partly through pressure from parents. Improved laboratory accommodation had been, or was being, provided; yet science rarely entered into the curriculum of the classical boy. Indeed, those who took science generally had to pay an extra fee for it, though I note one school in which science could be taken without apparatus or experiment at no extra charge. (Incidentally I may recall to you that quite recently a voice capable of making itself heard has been recommending for some boys science teaching divorced from experiment and observation.) It was still believed that a foreign language could only be taught by a foreigner, and the French lesson was still apt to be interrupted by many a Boeotian jest or to be regarded as a quiet time in which the week's tale of Latin verses could be completed. Latin was included in every boy's time-table, and any scientist or mathematician bound for Oxford or Cambridge had to face the hurdle of Greek. History had established itself, but it was not unusual for a boy on the Classical side to be confined to the history of Greece and Rome throughout his time at school, and on that side also English language and literature together with Geography might find no place in the timetable. Art and Manual Instruction were extras and all musical activities took place out of school.

So much for the curriculum. Of the organisation it is enough to say that it was, in most schools, very simple. The school was divided from top to bottom into sides— generally two, but sometimes three. It is also important to note that the Modern side existed mainly for the benefit of scientists and mathematicians. The conception of what is now sometimes called a Modern Studies course—a combination of history and languages—had hardly come into existence. In addition an Army class or Army side was recruited from boys of fifteen or so. Promotion was terminal and the School Certificate examination had not yet come into existence.

The first landmark I should fix in the story of development and change was the abolition of Greek as a compulsory subject for entrants to the older Universities. This not only led to a reduction in the number of boys taking that language, but it also made things easier on the Modern sides of public schools since the scientists no longer had to learn Greek cribs by heart at the age of eighteen; and it favoured the development of German, but the importance of German to boys intending to read for honours in Science at a University had not yet been realised.

In the matter of organisation, the next important change to be noticed is a gradual modification of the arrangement of the sides. In a number of schools these disappeared: where they were retained, the division was not carried through the whole school, but began after a year or so had been given by most boys to a common curriculum. This also was facilitated by the abolition of compulsory Greek, and perhaps indirectly by the institution in 1917 of the School Certificate Examination. The taking of this examination naturally tended to become a turning-point in a boy's career and was more and more used as a gateway to the Upper Fifth or Lower Sixth Forms. Although that examination is certainly not invulnerable to criticism, yet it has clearly had good results in regulating the course of work in the middle and lower parts of public schools.

A distinguishing feature, mentioned just now, of the organisation in public schools has been the system of terminal promotions. That system is difficult to avoid in schools which take in boys in large numbers not once a year, but three times a year. The special advantage claimed for it is that boys can more easily than under the system of annual promotions proceed up the school at a pace suited to their own rate of development. It has, however, a grave drawback in that it makes a continuous and progressive course of instruction difficult in all subjects, and in some subjects, Science for example, practically impossible. It has also led to the creation of a large number of forms at the bottom of the school, so that while the agile-minded boys leap up swiftly by double removes, the slower climb by short steps so numerous that by the time they reach the stage of the School Certificate Examination they are having to shave three times a week. A further disadvantage has been that the bright boys pass through the hands of a large number of masters spending perhaps no more than a term with each, until they reach the Sixth Form. It is not therefore surprising to find a growing tendency in schools to regulate movement through the forms in such a way that in the year, or in the two years, preceding the School Certificate Examination there is as little promotion as possible. Also below that point the number of steps or grades tends to be reduced in such a way that the majority of boys reach the examination stage in not more than three years after entry to the school.

In the teaching of modern languages there has been a gradual improvement. As to the causes of the change I confess to not being very certain, but credit is due to a group of pioneers who advocated what is known as the Direct Method and to the example set by the state-aided secondary schools. Furthermore, there has been a strong demand from the community for more instruction and better instruction in foreign languages. This improvement particularly affected work on the Modern sides of public schools, and as the teaching of history came to be based on different conceptions through the work of such teachers as Warner at Harrow, Marten at Eton, and, perhaps above all, Sanderson at Oundle, the Modern Studies course of which I spoke just now was able to be realised. It would be possible, if time were available, to trace gradual improvements—or at least changes— in the teaching of practically all the subjects, but from this list I am afraid that the names of English and Geography among main subjects would have to be withheld, since I am thinking now of the state of things as it was nineteen or twenty years ago.

The claims of Science to increased attention had been asserting themselves with increasing vehemence ever since the days of Spencer and Huxley. The first change to be remarked is that the practice of charging an extra fee for this subject was gradually abandoned—though a school could be mentioned in which it was still in force within the last three years. Of the branches of Science, Chemistry and Physics held the field until quite recently. Biology was indeed taken in a fair number of schools but only as a rule by those boys generally known as the First M.B.-sters. The introduction of the subject on anything like a large scale is of very recent date, but I note that at Oundle the importance of it was recognised many years ago by Sanderson. Finally, at this moment the cry is being raised for General Science—which may mean that Science is becoming more philosophical.

These changes and developments gave rise to two problems of a truly formidable nature. The first was the problem of the specialist teacher, the second the problem of what has been called the squeeze of subjects.

A distinctive feature of most public schools is—or was—a strong belief in the influence of the form-master. A form-master taught a group of boys for the greater part of their school time. This was easy when the boys gave so much of their time to the Classics with perhaps a little History, but it became more difficult as the curriculum grew in scope and as it was realised that not even the born teacher could cope with Latin, Greek, Modern History, French, and Geography—still less so when Science and Mathematics were added. There must be specialists, and more and more subjects came under the specialist régime. The dangers of that régime are serious. If I may for a moment stray outside the path of my discourse, it is interesting that in a few grant-earning secondary schools where specialisation has been taken to greater lengths than in public schools, an attempt has been made to combat its evils by re-introducing the tutorial system in one form or another. In the public schools it is generally speaking true to say that on the Classical side the form-master keeps in his hands at least the so-called English subjects and on the Modern side some other group of more or less cognate subjects.

As to the squeeze of subjects, a selection had to be made. How was it made? As has already been said, Latin was necessary for all boys who were likely to wish to go to one of the older Universities—which in effect meant the great majority. Even if a boy did not go to Oxford or Cambridge, it was held that Latin was educationally valuable for him. Again, to leave out a modern language was inconceivable. So far there was little or no choice. But how to choose among other subjects? Frankly, what answer was given I do not know—probably different answers in different schools, but so far as any general statement may be hazarded, there has been a tendency to take Greek out of the time-table of the lowest forms, substituting Art and increasing the time given to English subjects. Above the lowest forms a boy may have to choose whether he shall take Greek or German or Science. If he wishes to continue Art he must find the time outside class-room hours. The classics have been robbed to find more time for English and perhaps for Geography. Music and Manual Instruction continue to be leisure occupations.

A word falls to be said about the existence of vocational elements in the curriculum. There is a sense in which the mere idea of vocational training is abhorrent to the philosophy of public schools, based as that philosophy is on Greek ideals. And yet there was the Army class. It is true that no specifically military subjects were introduced there (I am thinking of days before Certificate A), but in it the liberal arts were studied in anything but a liberal spirit. Listen to Stalky—'This ain't your silly English Literature, you ass. It's our marks.' I note one interesting form of vocationalism in a certain public school which years ago had a class specially preparing boys for life in the colonies and dominions. They learnt to use a forge and to mend saddles. Another school had a class for boys intending to go to sea and a third had—and still has, I believe—an agricultural Sixth Form. The tendency through the period has been to attempt to abolish Army sides and to retain a special class only for Woolwich boys, sometimes not even for them. This was made possible through changes in the Army Entrance Examination. Engineering classes are few and show at present no signs of increasing. On the other hand more and more schools are establishing at the Sixth Form level a curriculum thought likely to be useful for boys who will be entering commercial life immediately after leaving school. This is sometimes

called the General Sixth, sometimes the Economics Sixth—
there are other names also. Here, as a rule, no specifically
commercial subjects are taught—such as Book-keeping,
Accountancy, Typewriting, and Shorthand. The idea is to
study not technique, as it were, but general problems.

Hitherto, in public schools, as in all secondary schools, there
has existed what might be termed a hierarchy of subjects—a
kind of order of merit in which Geography, Art, Music, and
Manual Instruction have occupied the lowest grades. But a
change is coming. The fact that in Art and Music the emotions
are more strongly engaged used to be a reason for grave
distrust on the part of schoolmasters: but in our day that
very fact is, to a growing number of minds, the best reason
for encouraging these activities. Unquestionably more
attention is being paid to them and in many places the results
are as surprising as they are gratifying. The neglect of
Geography in the past has certainly not been due to fears
concerning its effect on the emotions, but in the main I think
to sheer ignorance. On the whole, even to-day few public
schools seem to realise what an excellent school subject this
is, but I could name at least two among the more famous
schools where Geography has gained a place of honour.
Indeed, one might go much further and say that these two
schools have made contributions of the highest value to the
study of the subject.

English indeed is in a slightly better case than Geography.
Not so many public schoolmasters now as in former days
look upon it as 'a subject you can't really teach'. In those
days when it appeared on the time-table at all, it consisted
of lessons in grammar and also the learning by heart and the
reciting—in a surly growling monotone—of a tale of
English verses. But by degrees it came to be realised that,
for example, Latin Prose is not the best way of teaching the
art of expression to a boy who cannot translate into Latin
'Balbus built a wall' without making two or three grammatical blunders, and that detention school or punishment

school is not the most effective means for promoting ortho-graphy. And there are a few public schools in which it is realised that the speaking of verse is an art. On the whole, however, progress in this branch of teaching has been slower than in others. And perhaps that is not to be wholly imputed as a fault, since of all school subjects English Language and Literature presents the teacher with the thorniest problems, and there are so many voices crying aloud Lo here! and Lo there!

Here this brief and imperfect sketch of the history of development in the last thirty years must draw to a close. As to what the future may bring it would be dangerous to speak at length or in any detail. One general tendency may be discussed which is likely to spread and to have important results. In the past the curriculum has been based on the assumption that certain subjects of instruction are more valuable than others and must be attempted by all: in other words the boy was fitted to the curriculum. More and more we are coming to stress the fact that the curriculum must be fitted to the boy or to homogeneous groups of boys. Out of such considerations new combinations of subjects may come into being—for example, it may be found that many boys will benefit from a curriculum with only one foreign language, with increased time for English, for History, and for Geography; Mathematics reduced in scope; General Science introduced; and a good dose of activities which train hand and eye to work together. Furthermore, it may be prophesied that the school library will be more freely and intelligently used and that there will be certain lesson times in which boys can decide, under guidance, how they shall occupy themselves. But whether my forecast is right or wrong, I hope at least that it may have been made clear that there has been in public schools continuous and lively develop-ment in the last few years and no sign at all of that com-placency which runs before the decline and fall of any kind of human endeavour.

EDUCATION AND MORALITY

Oswald Schwarz

In the course of our educational work we ask of children a great number of things which are unpleasant to them, or even, as we say, contrary to their nature. We want them to work when they want to play, not to do the things which they like doing, to concentrate when they want to relax, to obey when they want to be free, and so on. The point is, to which part of the child's personality are we appealing when we expect him to comply with these demands? Are they forcibly imposed upon him or is there some kind of instinct in the child which meets our demands half-way? Is it the much-praised moral sense? Does something of the kind actually exist, and if so, is it an intrinsic feature of the child's personality, or is it the product of our education? An answer to these most disconcerting and disquieting questions is the purpose of this paper.

I am by no means prepared to commit myself to any ready-made definition of morality—at least, not yet. It will suffice to say that there are two kinds of phenomena that compose our moral life—Morality, in the strict sense of the word, and Ethics. By Morality I mean the whole set of demands and prohibitions sanctioned by tradition and generally accepted by society, which a member of this society has to accept indisputably like the rules of a game: in other words, things which 'should' be done. By Ethics I mean the original sense of an 'ought' and the deep-seated awareness that there are eternal values, far beyond any temporal moral code, values which we ought to realise, to materialise, and to incorporate into our spiritual existence in order to become fully awakened human beings.

This reluctance to embark on a discussion on the very idea

of Morality is justifiable in that it is solely the psychological aspect of the problem in which we are interested. Developmental psychology has already collected a great number of facts concerning the moral conduct and ethical attitude at every stage of the child's development, and I am now going, quite roughly, to outline this development. Our knowledge of these exact data makes it possible for us to draw some conclusions about the educational measures adequate to the various phases and the widely different moral capacity of children, and requisite to their difficulties and problems, which likewise undergo continual change.

From this psychological point of view the difference between Morality and Ethics presents itself in a new light. Morality seems to imply a mode of conduct, forcibly imposed on the child from without, whereas the ethical sense represents a real product of, and an essential element in, his personality. Although this difference actually exists, at least in principle, it would be incorrect, perhaps even unfair, to say that moral conduct is quite alien to human nature, or that it is only his own helplessness that makes the child submit, or rather succumb, to the various moral commands. But it is true—and the importance of this fact can hardly be overrated, that the child's nature, both his psychological and biological needs, really meet the moral order half-way, and that moral conduct satisfies a definite need in him and safeguards a normal and healthy development.

I

The very first moral phenomena we meet are a striking proof of this contention, which might seem strange at first sight. Moral education begins on the first day of life when we train the child to regular meal-times. I call this measure a moral one because it introduces into the child's life the principle of order, and the principle of order is a moral principle of paramount importance. To keep order is the fundamental condition of social life, the basic element in any kind of work and creation: in submitting to order we realise and accept the fact of objective laws overruling the inconsistency of our subjective wants, and this notion leads to the first conception of the idea of authority.

It would seem only too obvious that this keeping order is something forcibly imposed on the child, utterly contrary to his nature, and yet just the reverse is true. A child's nature meets this demand more than half-way; it requires order as the guarantee of harmonious development. In the first place, the small child is a highly social being; it seeks every possible contact with grown-ups, tries eagerly to fit into the community of the family, every condition of which it willingly accepts, and regards exclusion from this group as the worst punishment. Secondly, the child wants and needs above all safety and security, and nothing can provide this better and more fully than order and a definite frame of life to which he can adhere almost pedantically. To have experienced security is the indispensable condition of acquiring later on the right sense of freedom. Freedom implies the utmost insecurity, and without this background of previous security, freedom degenerates into licence.

2

Towards the end of his second year the child enters upon one of the most difficult periods of his life. He now discovers his Ego; that is to say, he realises that he is an individual, distinct from any other; that he is no longer only an element in the family, but a real member. 'Here am I, and there—separated as by an abyss—are the others.' That is the tragic formula which flings wide open the door to all the problems of human existence.

This sense of being an individual manifests itself first of all in having a will of one's own. The child now begins to plan and design his own actions, and is most anxious to carry them out in his own way. All too often his will and plans clash with those of his environment, and conflicts are inevitable. Thus, he experiences for the first time the hardship of life. An almost amusing sense of honour and the first touching signs of shame are facets of the new-born personality. Oddly enough, at the very same time, the sociability of the child reaches its acme: at no time, either before or after —at least not during the next ten or fifteen years—is he more anxious to bridge this gulf between himself and others. The gregarious instinct, as we may call infantile sociability, changes now into a sort of individual affection, which attracts and attaches the child to individual persons, whether of his own age, or adults. Tenderness, sympathy, jealousy, envy are products and manifestations of this new kind of relationship.

With regard to our problem, it is most important to realise that all these emotions and attitudes, such as a sense of honour, shame, pity, envy, obstinacy, etc., are anything but moral, still less ethical phenomena. They are not 'achievements', as real moral and ethical actions are; they are simply and solely biological products, reactions, wants, and needs of the child's nature, all or most of them disappearing again when progressing development produces new products, reactions, needs, and wants. Nothing would be more useless than to appeal to this sense of honour, nothing more wounding than to neglect or ridicule this chivalry, comic as it sometimes is; nothing more detrimental than to try to break the obstinacy and counteract the child's plans. All this will make it clear why we call this age a particularly difficult one. Two strongly antagonistic tendencies are developed, and the child is torn between his passionate need for contact and his equally strong need for self-preservation. And the conflict is pathetic because both these tendencies are needs, real biological phenomena which overtake the child; and as he does not yet possess any moral capacity for coping with this conflict, he is in danger of being drowned and needs understanding help from without.

How can this help be given? This birth of the child's personality, lighting up a soul where before existed only a creature—this awareness of himself produces a corresponding change in our attitude towards him. So far we have only nursed and trained a living being, from now onwards we have to educate a human child. What is the idea, aim, and means of education at this age? The world in which the child is still exclusively living, the medium in which he is embedded and through which all influence from without reaches him, is represented by contact with other human beings. And this medium must be saturated with love, kindness, and approval. The child is not yet capable of distinguishing right from wrong, but he senses the slightest shadow clouding the friendliness of this atmosphere. Obedience has as yet no moral sense, it simply means pleasing somebody. It will be six or seven years before he has a proper conception of justice, and some fifteen years before this conception corresponds to the abstract idea of an ethical value. And yet at the stage we are considering, the child is already possessed by a sense of injustice, but to him injustice means lack of love. Education at this age and for many years afterwards is, as we have seen, not so much an activity as an attitude, namely, the capacity to create the suitable atmosphere. In addition to this, one sort of activity is of course necessary, that is to say, firmness and consistency. If we have asked a child to do something, we must insist firmly on its being done, and on the other hand, nothing must weaken the consistency of our asking. This kindness combined with firmness—an attitude which may be described as 'educational love' provides the child with what he most needs—security—and creates confidence. Confidence, in the form of self-confidence, is the main source of any kind of efficiency in after life, and confidence in the educator paves the way to the idea and acceptance of authority. An educator who has failed to create this confidence has not only discredited himself and the very idea of education, but has definitely diverted, and that all too often, the moral development of the child from its normal course. I have no hesitation in saying that the

many asocial features, such as distrust, diffidence, aggress-
iveness, argumentativeness, scepticism, arrogance, shyness,
and the like, which cause so much annoyance in school and
conflicts in after life, can be traced back to the initial failure
to develop confidence.

3

The great emotional upheaval of this phase gradually sub-
sides in six months or so, and a fresh interest comes to the
fore, that of manipulating material, in other words, playing.
A great deal of effort has been devoted to the study of child-
play, with the result that we now fully realise the outstanding
importance of this activity. And it is by no means an ex-
aggeration to say that a child who has not learnt to play
properly will find great difficulty in learning how to work.

By 'playing' we mean an activity where the stress lies on
the process, on the doing as such, where no result is intended
and therefore no essential end exists. A playing child piles
up bricks indefinitely, fills receptacles with masses of sand,
covers innumerable sheets of paper with his scribbling, and
so on, whereas 'working' is the deliberate effort to create a
new entity. Here the activity no longer consists of mere
doing, but is entirely directed by the intended result; it is
premeditated and designed, and comes to an essential end
when the result is obtained. Between the age of $1\frac{1}{2}$ and 6 play
gradually changes into work. In the intermediary stages,
first the child becomes aware of the unintentional effect of
his play, e.g. that blocks piled one upon another do not
collapse; then he gives this product a name, 'this is a house';
finally, he becomes proud of his accomplishment: 'Look here,
look what I have done.'

Sooner or later, but inevitably, in every nursery between
the ages of $3\frac{1}{2}$ and 5, a scene like this happens. The child is
absorbed in his play; the mother asks him to do something
else, e.g. to go with her for a walk, but the child answers:
'Wait a moment, I must finish this *first*.' Many an in-

experienced mother takes this for disobedience or even obstinacy. How mistaken she is! In reality, this inconspicuous incident, those few words of refusal signify a peak of our development almost unsurpassed in importance. The words 'I must finish this first' actually mean: 'It must be—or wants to be—finished'; in other words, the child discovers for the first time a kind of *demand* which the work itself imposes on him, a demand which he willingly accepts, fulfils, and to which he submits. In this demand we easily recognise what we call *duty*, and so the simple product of play-work has now acquired the characteristics of a *task*, inasmuch as 'task' means 'there is something which must be done', and 'duty' means '*I* have got to do it'. *This moment is the birthday of the ethical sense.* The child has grasped that there is an intrinsic command from without, and a response in himself which makes him accept and obey it.

The far-reaching importance of this step in our develop-ment can hardly be over-emphasised, as all the elements in our capacity for work, e.g. interest, concentration, pursuing an aim, overcoming difficulties, etc., are its ultimate outcome. It is necessary to give only one example: An extensive investigation has shown that 80 per cent of the junior school-children tested who failed to pass the first grade, did so because they had not acquired this work-attitude during their play-development before coming to school. From the theoretical point of view it is important to note that the child has quite spontaneously made this discovery at a certain stage of his maturation, that the notion of duty and a task is a genuine product, a genuine manifestation of child-growth, in fact, almost a product of nature. But it is not the result of education, not imposed from without, not taught. On the contrary, the more anxious we are to 'teach' this sense of duty, the more we bar its spontaneous development, and these noisy attempts only deafen the child's ear to the soft and gentle call of the work itself. The paramount importance that these exact psychological facts contribute to our problem is evidence that the ethical sense is an intrinsic feature of our nature, that we are ethical in so far as we are human.

With a normal child the development of his capacity for work and duty should be finished by the age of six. He is then prepared and mature for school. At roughly the same time he makes another discovery, one which we may term 'moral value'.

We have already said that the small child is not yet able to distinguish right from wrong, but that his moral barometer, if we may call it that, is the reaction of grown-ups to his actions. If this reaction is unfavourable, he becomes unhappy. At the stage with which we are now dealing, such an unfavourable reaction of grown-ups creates something entirely new in the child: not merely unhappiness or unpleasantness, but a feeling of general unworthiness which soon crystallises into a sense of *guilt*. This sense of guilt is still diffuse, vague, and unqualified: I 'feel' unworthy or guilty, is what the child feels, but he cannot turn this into an objective feeling by knowing I 'am' guilty, because I have 'done' this or that. This last step towards acquiring moral conscience has to be helped by education: the moral sense is a product of nature, the association of this sense with a particular deed is the result of culture. That is why there is only one morality and so many morals.

Although a child already possesses at this age a sense of duty and guilt, it is useless to appeal to these moral qualities in the course of our educational work, because they are not yet far enough developed for him to make deliberate use of them. He is still more in their grip, or more possessed by them than possessing them; he is still more victim than master of his morality.

How entirely emotionally and how little rationally children of this age react may be learnt from a closer study of the development of self-criticism and the effect of criticism by others. Not before the age of nine are children capable of objective self-criticism: not till then can they see their work as it really is. Up to this age a child invariably finds all he produces perfect and beautiful, and cannot conceive that anybody could think otherwise of his achievements. Hence school reports, especially unfavourable ones, have no effect whatever on him.

4

The picture changes entirely when we approach the next period of the age from eight to eleven approximately. The tide of emotional strain and ethical discoveries has gradually receded. The child enters into a state of pronounced realism, in which intellect takes the lead. Whereas his world so far has mainly consisted of human beings, he now discovers, so to speak, the world of matter. His main and predominant interest now is to find his bearings in this new and strange world, he wants to understand and know what is going on around him, to intrude into and conquer this strangeness. And because knowledge—knowledge of what things are like, how they are made, how they work—is not only the best, but actually the only, means to this end, we find children of this age anxious to learn, actually more so than at any other time of life.

This attitude has now important reactions on the child's moral status. He realises that the world of nature and culture is ruled and worked by firmly established objective laws, that there is a purpose and intention in everything. This discovery results in a fresh strengthening of the realisation of objectivity, which, to my mind at least, lies at the bottom of any moral attitude, and from which proceeds a further reinforcement of aim and the sense of duty. The outcome and, so to speak, moral aspect or version of this strong sense of realism is an almost fanatical worship of truth in its most elementary conception: 'true' meaning that which is real.

How does all this come about? Are we to assume a strong push in development in the moral sphere as such? The answer is decidedly No: or, to put it more carefully, Certainly not in the first place. The underlying cause is a biological one. It is the intensive development of a child's physique that provides him with an overwhelming and irresistible sense of strength and power that excites him and enables this advance into reality. And all these 'moral' characteristics are just irradiations or reflections of this vitality on to the moral sphere or, as one might say, biological facts described in moral terms. It is not because it is moral and good, but because it is necessary and useful for the purpose of conquest that a child of this age is most eager to learn.

Something similar takes place in the ethical sphere. Children of this age are almost obsessed by a sense of honour and justice. The sense of honour is always coupled with a sense of strength—at least the gallant, almost quixotic, sense of honour we meet with at this age. By 'just' these children simply mean what is real, lawful, almost practical. The phrase 'morals of virility' perhaps best sums up this attitude.

An almost infallible proof of this interpretation is the reaction of such children to educational influences. An appeal to their 'moral' qualities has very little, if any, effect, because the moral element in these attitudes has hardly any driving power. Similarly, a particular type of educator, or special capacities in the educator, are now required, quite distinct from those in the preceding phase. Again it is the virile man, the man who knows everything and can do everything, that appeals most to these children. Whilst it was in the preceding phase the personality of the educator, it is now the capabilities of the teacher that command the greatest respect. He is expected to be a reliable guide in the unknown territory that opens before the eyes of the young explorers. It is clear from all this, that this age is less susceptible than any other to any kind of authoritarian influence. Conquerors may abide by laws and accept, or even like, discipline in so far as it is a means to their ends, but they do not tolerate personal interference. It requires great tact, skill, and superiority to cope with this age.

5

This period of concentrated strength brings childhood to a close and is immediately followed by puberty—the most troubled phase of our life. From the peak of vitality the child is plunged into a whirlpool of strange sensations and conflicting emotions, emerging after years of struggle into an entirely new being—a personality. It is indeed difficult for the child to go through this period, and difficult, perhaps for the same reason, for the psychologist to describe it. For our purpose this much may suffice: Development during childhood may be imagined as taking place on one plane only; from puberty onwards it becomes three-dimensional, corresponding to three new discoveries of the adolescent. The *first* discovery is the conception of *time*. As a child, he lived only in the present, but from now on he looks back upon his childhood as upon something that is past, and learns to look forward to the 'future' as something to come. The 'moral' equivalent of this new orientation in life is the conception of an *aim*. The *second* discovery is the definite formation of an *Ego*, an experience which, viewed from a moral angle, contrasts the individual with others, including him at the same time into human society in a new and special way. The result is the conception of the *fellow-being* with all its moral implications. The *third* discovery is the idea of a super-material world, the *realm of spiritual ideas and values, the real ethical sphere.*

By these three discoveries the foundation of the ethical personality is laid to which further development adds nothing essentially new. At this stage, the youth becomes what we may call ethically productive; he apprehends the idea of ethical values. 'True' no longer means 'that which is real', as he thought at the age of ten; 'right' is not merely that which serves a purpose; 'honour' no more the outcome of strength and vigour, but truth, right and honour, etc. are now conceived as objective 'ideas', completely devoid of any materialistic sense or practical application. Just as ten years ago the child suddenly felt in himself an echo to the demand imposed upon him by his work, and responded to the call by developing the idea of duty, so now the adolescent hears the call of these values, and responds by developing the higher equivalent of duty: responsibility.

In the concept of duty, the whole emphasis lies on the objective side. Duty means that there is something outside us that wants, and therefore has, to be done, whereas in the state of responsibility, a subjective initiative meets this call from without. We obey or submit to duty, but we accept and shoulder responsibility. Duty is a term belonging to the moral sphere, responsibility to the ethical. There is an exceedingly fine remark by T. F. Coade to the effect that responsibility is derived from responsiveness. How useless and dangerous it is to expect responsibility from children before they have developed the consciousness of an Ego.

It is a dangerous and frightening adventure on which the adolescent embarks. No wonder he needs some help, someone to lean on. Once more the educator is called upon, this time in the form of a 'leader'. In the first period, he was, as we shall remember, just the protective power, the creator of an atmosphere, the embodiment of love and kindness; in the second phase, he appeared as an instructor, a transmitter of knowledge, in both cases a functionary rather than an individual; in this period a particular individual is chosen for his individuality, which means that he personifies one of these values, standing for an ideal great or humble, ranging from an all-round hero to a meticulous entomologist. But he must stand for it. His very existence is then felt as a guarantee that it is possible to put into practice the kind of life which the adolescent, in his constant inner struggles, has dimly conceived and vaguely designed. The leader shows the road and points to the goal.

6

It may be well to sum up. Throughout childhood morality dominates, consisting in the acceptance of, and submission to, the powers of the practical world. These powers consist of laws, ruling the realm of matter and of human society. Routine and habit, the need of security, the wish to please his human surroundings, and the urge to understand and conquer the world around him are the chief sources from which spring the child's compliance with these laws, that signify his 'moral' attitude.

The existence of ethics dawns on the child in the shape of duty, when he first discovers the idea of work, and conceives the demand of the work to be accomplished and finished. Although the succeeding years contribute some parts of the ethical development (justice, truth, honour, etc.) one may say that ethical consciousness and awareness do not become essential and predominant until adolescence.

The moral and ethical senses are phenomena, parts, products of human life; and hence we may, or rather must, ask what function they have, what purpose they serve. The answer can easily be drawn from all the empirical facts in our sketch of the child's development. Both the ethical and moral senses are means of grasping the existence of laws. In much the same way as we perceive with our physical senses the existence of material reality, by means of sight the existence of light and colour, by means of hearing the existence of sound, so we grasp by means of the moral sense the existence of moral codes, by means of the ethical sense the existence of values. Therefore, we can speak respectively of a moral or ethical 'sense' in the strictest meaning of the term. They have a cognitive function. As senses or capacities, as one may say, they are intrinsic parts of our nature; we 'are' moral as far as, or because, we are human beings. If proofs of this very obvious fact are required, our analysis can provide us with one. It is most significant that during the course of development the moral and ethical capacities appear in close connection with biological conditions. The feebleness and helplessness of the small child, and his social instinct, dispose him to the acceptance of moral demands, and the ethical achievements of the ten-year-old child are manifestations of his greatly increased vitality. There is one more interesting fact which we may mention, in passing, as another proof of our contention. The full development of our physical sensual capacities, sight and hearing, is closely linked up with, and largely dependent on, the development of an ethical capacity, namely, the sense of beauty. Without the idea of beauty our physical functions are incomplete, but, conversely, beauty cannot be apprehended to the full with an imperfect sensuality.

Morality and ethics are responses to calls; morality answers the social, ethics the spiritual call. There is yet a third capacity which, although distinctly different from the other two, belongs to the same category: Religiousness. The religious 'sense' furnishes the idea of God and answers the call from Him. It is this sense that provides the cognition of the absolute.

Although profoundly different in kind, morality and ethics must co-operate because both are parts of our existence. The shortest possible description of this co-operation is as follows: Morality involves limitation, all moral statements are prohibiting and forbidding: 'You must not'! This limitation would be unbearable and undignified: the permanent control in the realm of facts is acceptable only because of the liberating effect of our ethical sense. Through it we are allowed an unlimited expansion of existence into the realm of spirit, thus experiencing real freedom. In this idea of freedom, which is really controlled power, culminates the co-operation of morality and ethics, which constitute the very idea of humanity.

To awaken, cultivate, and preserve this spirit of freedom is the means and task of moral education.

THE CRISIS OF FREEDOM IN EDUCATION

F. Clarke

W E live in an age when freedom can no longer be taken for granted, nor regarded, as twenty-five or thirty years ago, as a good lying ready to hand if we are but prepared to take it up. Doubts are even expressed whether freedom is the thing men desire at all to-day when once they have caught a glimpse of its obligations and responsibilities. If, then, we are to go on with the effort of spreading and sustaining a doctrine of freedom in a world which may become increasingly in-different to it, or even hostile as change takes place in the order of precedence in which men range their ruling values, it would seem advisable to make some effort to re-think our situation in terms not only of present actuality, but of future possibility, so far as that can be estimated.

It is to some reflections upon the necessity for such re-thinking and the conditions under which it must proceed that I propose to address myself here.

The issues cut deep, to the roots of life itself. For, as a distinguished French writer remarks: 'There have never been any crises of education. The crises of education are not crises of education, they are crises of life.' In such a crisis we are now deeply immersed, and a little later on I shall suggest some reasons for the feeling that English people are, in some ways, not well placed to appreciate adequately either its intensity or its depth. Hence all the more reason for con-centrating our attention upon it now, and for trying to probe into the *conditions* which, in a time of crisis such as this, must be recognised by all consistent advocates of freedom in education.

For my present purpose I do not propose to regard the

crisis as constituted by nothing more than what is being called to-day 'the challenge of the dictatorships'. To do that is not only to over-simplify the problem but to *externalise* it; or, as the psycho-analyst might say, to 'project' it and so come to see it where it is not. There is always something comforting in this process of externalising or 'projecting', in the thought that we have got Satan—most probably our own Satan—into the open as it were, so that we can slam at him without reserve. The phenomenon is common enough to-day and accounts no doubt for a widespread recourse to violence in the modern world, a violence which usually seems to find for itself some pseudo-sanctification.

The problem is, in reality, much nearer home, so far as we are concerned, though I have no wish to underestimate the reality and the seriousness of the challenge of the dictatorships. I wish only to suggest that to externalise our problem wholly is to encourage false ideas about *ourselves* and our own conditions, and perhaps to give encouragement to a propensity to be virtuous with the other man's temptations while effectively screening the realities of our own. We ought indeed to be very sure of ourselves before we settle down in the comforting belief that this island of ours is a sort of Gideon's fleece, destined to remain bone-dry while all around is wet with the dews of change.

It is of the crisis *within* therefore that I wish to speak, of the crisis within ourselves, little as we may be conscious of it as yet.

Two questions at once suggest themselves. In the first place, do men really *desire* freedom to-day with a full sense of all that it means, the responsibilities, the constant vigilance within and without that self-sovereignty demands, the readiness to make the burdens of the community one's own, and the *tension* which true freedom always brings with it? For freedom may be rather a terrible thing in its ultimate demands. It is at any rate a high achievement rather than an easy gift, and an achievement which does not guarantee itself, but calls for unceasing alertness and vigilance to sustain it.

There are those to-day who would call attention to the increasing matter-of-factness of life, to the growing disposition to seek and be content with very earthly satisfactions, to the decreasing tension of ideal striving, and to the widespread desire for a strong state as the guarantor both of security and of the very material satisfactions which, it is alleged, men are more and more seeking. The ideal of Bishop Blougram, we are told, is enough—'This hutch shall rustle with sufficient straw'. I am not prepared to say that this is so, though the rating of values in this regard does seem to have changed considerably since even the late Victorian days. I would only suggest that, if it is so to any degree, we have in this alone a strong argument for re-thinking our position.

But for the purpose of this address the second question is much more relevant. Put crudely, it is this: Are we ourselves under some illusion as to the nature and conditions of our own freedom? May we not be quite unconsciously taking for granted some highly favourable factors here in our own peculiar English situation which give us the feeling of a freedom for which we have not paid the full price, and might, perhaps, be unwilling to pay if the full price were exacted? Is there some unacknowledged security or defence or *cushion*, if you like, which is, in fact, carrying a large share of the responsibility for us, limiting the degree of our exposure, and so giving us an illusion of a freedom to which no sustaining effort of our own corresponds? In other words, have we thought the thing right through to a full appreciation of all that it involves, apart from the accidents of English good fortune, and accepted it with open-eyed realisation of what it means?

Or are we like some young pacifists I have met who adopt pacifist principles with the unexamined assumption that the rest of life will go on as usual, cared for by somebody else: the milk and the newspaper will be at the door every morning, the policeman about his duty, and the sought-for job and economic security available when needed?

It is upon this question that I would lay the main emphasis. Are we fully aware, on the one hand, of the *conditions*, and on the other hand of the *responsibilities* of freedom, ready with all our strength to sustain and apply the one, and to produce a type which can accept and sustain the full burden of the other? Or are we, as a matter of fact, accepting as the real thing a measure of freedom which is much more narrowly conditioned than we realise, and so, possibly, producing a type which is less securely based in itself and more vulnerable to the attacks of what Plato calls Theft, Witchcraft, and Violence, than we should have thought likely?

It may be that, when we have examined the matter, we shall be ready to accept as our English form of freedom the relatively limited thing which it may turn out to be. But if so, we ought to know what we are doing, and not be using language about freedom in education that is incompatible with the surrounding framework of conditions which, it is presumed, we should wish to retain.

In the hope that, by so doing, I may make my point a little more clear, let me quote a couple of sentences from the well-know book of my honoured friend and predecessor, Sir Percy Nunn's *Education: its Data and First Principles*. Speaking of that which should constitute the central purpose of all education and endow it with full human significance, he says: 'We shall stand throughout on the position that nothing good enters into the human world except in and through the free activities of individual men and women, and that educational practice should be shaped to accord with that truth.' And again: 'Freedom is, in truth, the condition, if not the source, of all the higher goods. Apart from it duty has no meaning, self-sacrifice no value, authority no sanction.' May I now clarify my point by saying that I should accept as axiomatic these statements about the supremacy of the ideal of freedom both for life and education? But, especially at such a time as this and in view of the sharp concrete issues with which we may find ourselves faced before very long, I should feel that some questions have to be asked and answered before we can translate such principles into established practice. These questions would be such as:

(1) What are the necessary conditions of such freedom? In other words, what forms and degree of *submission*, of intelligent acceptance and *use* of conditions, are essential to the rich *self-assertion* which the goal of freedom seems to imply? For if freedom is an achievement, it must be *learned*, partly by the exercise of it in progressively higher forms and partly by steadily increasing knowledge and willing acceptance of its conditions. There is a promise that we shall be made free, but there is also a condition— 'Ye shall know the truth'.

(2) Is the freedom to be conceived of as absolute, accepting all the anarchism and disintegration that may mean, or is a given framework of life presupposed—the English social and cultural order for instance—limiting, defining, and canalising, as it were, this freedom?

(3) Still more fundamentally, if freedom is to be taken in an absolute sense, are we sure that we should be willing to accept the result of applying it in education as giving us what we thought we wanted? Or should we be, like King Midas, most uncomfortably embarrassed and disconcerted at getting what we believed to be our desire? I have noted, occasionally, utterances on this matter of freedom which have raised precisely this doubt in my mind. What would the writer or speaker say if he really achieved what he declares himself to be aiming at? Surely, we do need to clear our minds on these great matters and to remember always that the world in which we have to live and work is many-sided, complicated and most disconcertingly bent on having its own say in the achievement of human ends. It is in such a world that education goes on, and we need to know a good deal about it before we can be sure that we accept in all its concrete bearings and

forms of expression some abstract principle in which we claim to believe. In my South African days I have known men who claimed to believe wholly in the principle of instruction for all children through the medium of the mother-tongue, and yet resisted straightforward applications of the principle when they saw what it meant in the concrete.

Concerning such questions as these that I have raised about what we are to mean by freedom and its working out in practice, perhaps it will be relevant if I record here a few things that have struck me during the last three years of life and work in England after some twenty-four years of work oversea. I may be permitted to mention as a personal matter not wholly out of place here, that I am still unable to avoid a somewhat detached point of view in the observation of things English.

In the first place, while I have been struck by the progress and experiment in some of the more enlightened boarding schools, I am also struck by some other things. Am I right in supposing that most of these schools are *secure* places, generally secluded, well-equipped, and attended by the children of fairly well-to-do people who take a keen interest in the education of their offspring? While I have no doubt of the educational possibilities of such circumstances, I am left wondering how far freedom in such favouring conditions really carries one. How much of the strain and tension of it is borne by the circumstances rather than by the pupil? We should all like to see more of such experiments carried out in very different conditions, where less of the strain is borne by circumstance and more by the pupil. Such experiments are being made, I know, but I should like to see more of them.

I have heard it suggested that many English pupils suffer from under-exposure, from lack of raw-handed contact with real difficulty and even danger, with only their own resources to aid them. I do not know how true this is or whether there are cases where freedom is a sort of luxury which can be

enjoyed because circumstances have been so carefully pre-
arranged against mischance. But if this is so at all, perhaps
we need to take care not to exaggerate the degree to which
initiative and self-reliance and willingness to endure hardness
do actually 'transfer', as the psychologists say, from the
protected conditions of the school to the exposed conditions
of the world's life.

Canadian boys I have known seem often to have learned
this kind of lesson *out* of school, and there may well be some
tendency among us to exaggerate the degree of transfer of
the qualities of freedom from the school to the outer world.
Protection indeed there must be—that is implicit in the very
idea of education—but let us be fully aware of the fact, and
let us even ask ourselves whether, at times, we have not too
much of it.

Most of all, however, during these last three years I have
become aware of the enormous importance of what may be
called the 'taken for granted' in English life and education.
A distinguished American sociologist, writing the introduction to Karl Mannheim's book *Idealogy and Utopia*,
remarks: 'The most important thing we can know about a
man is what he takes for granted, and the most elemental
and important facts about a society are those that are seldom
debated and generally regarded as settled.'

The area of this 'taken for granted' region is particularly
wide in English life, and a great many, perhaps most, of the
most vital influences in education lie within it. This, if anything, is the distinguishing peculiarity of England, obvious
enough to anyone who has had close acquaintance with
societies where the most fundamental things are in question
and matter for passionate debate. Here the deposit of long
centuries of security and unbroken continuity, the product
of a social history which has been free to work out solutions
to its problems without serious threat of invasion from without or of irreconcilable cleavage within, has given this result:
that the processes of education on the one hand, and the pre-

suppositions of the social tradition on the other hand, are so intimately bound together, so much one thing, that it does not occur to us to set them explicitly in relation to one another. That, no doubt, is why we find it so difficult to explain to the foreigner how the thing is done. But I doubt whether there is any other country quite like ours in this regard, certainly not those countries whose tradition is still in the making, often under the stress of cleavage and conflict, nor those in a state of cultural upheaval.

It may be held that a state of things where the acceptance of fundamentals is so universal and so complete as not to need bringing to explicit consciousness at all is a most happy condition that ought not to be disturbed. But it may not lie with us in actual fact to decide whether it shall be disturbed or not. Indeed, there are even now some indications that we shall soon be forced to become much more explicit about these fundamentals than we have found it necessary to be hitherto. And, in any case, are we entitled to talk the language of a full-blooded freedom until we have explored this wide region of the 'taken for granted' and decided in what way we propose to take it into account?

Recently, I have found much illumination on this matter from a striking little pamphlet by a German writer, Adolf Löwe, now attached to the University of Manchester. It is published with the significant title *The Price of Liberty*, and in substance it is an acute enquiry into just these phenomena we are now discussing. The writer is well qualified by his sharply contrasted German experience to bring into vivid relief—perhaps too vivid—precisely those deeply rooted characteristics of English life which for most of us lie uninspected, perhaps even unsuspected, in the wide region of the 'taken for granted'.

Impressed by the marked freedom of movement and decision in English life the writer of the pamphlet was at first inclined to say: 'Here is a social milieu allowing every individual freely to indulge his impulses and capacities.' But very soon he is led to abandon this view and finds the key rather in a peculiar combination of self-restraint and social and mental conformity. 'The English type in all classes', he declares, 'lacks a certain last touch of individualisation.' *Conformity*, he finds, is the necessary pre-condition of such freedom as is permissible and 'every radical disturber of convention is punished with social ostracism'. In other words, if I may paraphrase, one of the highest and most powerful of the tribal gods goes by the name of 'It Isn't Done'.

Such conformity, our author feels, is self-created, and he drives home the point in a pregnant sentence. 'Conformity is, of course, a product of education, and all social institutions are focussed on its maintenance. But, if we disregard the handful of rebels, this conformity is felt not as a compulsion, but as the genuine form of self-realisation'. The point here is crucial and we must return to it.

I can permit myself only two more quotations from this highly significant analysis. The general conclusion is drawn in the words: 'A large scale society can stand the strain of freedom of action on the part of its members only if the individualisation of its members is kept within definite limits. The individual must pay for this freedom by being turned, to a certain extent, into a type. The price of liberalism as a social principle is the sacrifice of self-indulgence.'

In the last quotation I shall cite our author gets in a real home-thrust and definitely challenges the Englishman's idea that he, at any rate, is under no dictator. Speaking of the Englishman he says: 'His dictator is installed in his heart. He identifies himself with his code as the pious Jew identifies himself with the Law.'

In passing, we ought to note that, if it really is true that so powerful and all-embracing a discipline lies at the base of English freedom, we shall need to take a little care in defining the difference between ourselves and the totalitarians. Obviously, a simple-looking distinction like that between freedom and discipline will not do.

I have been attempting, in the preceding remarks, to give point to my suggestion that in the propagation in England of a doctrine of freedom in education there may be highly important conditioning factors that have not been taken sufficiently into account, that the kind of freedom we really seek may have peculiar characteristics of its own, and that the social and historical determinations and limitations which control our objective may be far more powerful and widely operative than we realise.

It would follow that, if this is so, we need to define very carefully our own position with comprehensive regard to *all* the factors involved, and to shake ourselves free once for all from any illusions that may still be clinging to our thought and practice. With, perhaps, some over-simplification of a highly complex matter might we say that the road to freedom can be followed under one or other of two banners, the one inscribed 'Pre-supposed Conformity', and the other 'Thoroughgoing Individualisation'? The English, it would seem, march under the first, the German pursuers of freedom under the second. Adolf Löwe, in the little book already quoted, brings out the distinction very clearly. Either, as he suggests we English do, we accept the conformity as a condition of the freedom, arguing, as perhaps we might, that the conformity involves no net loss of freedom if the alternative is an individualisation so thoroughgoing as to threaten social disintegration and render highly precarious any freedom at all that has any external implications. Or, alternatively, we can go the whole way with individualisation and take the consequences.

I should doubt very much whether, for most English people, there is really any choice between these alternatives. We have already chosen long ago, and are now committed by a long history to the first of them. Further, I should be disposed to question as both historically and philosophically unsound the procedure of setting conformity against freedom as a necessary price to be paid for the latter. On Löwe's view the freedom must fall within the conformity. But is there not good precedent for the counter view that the conformity falls within the freedom as a necessary condition and ingredient of it? Something like that might be our English answer if ever we took the trouble to become articulate about it. As Professor Hocking so justly points out, the social character of man is structural, not adhesive: that is, the social discipline is integral to the freedom. And even if we admit that the conformity *is* a subtraction from the freedom, we can still argue that the half-loaf with which we are left is better than no bread at all, which seems to be the practical issue of the pursuit of sheer individualisation to the uttermost in disregard of the social conditions of freedom.

But though we may not be forced to choose between the two alternatives, it is most important to recognise that they exist. Still more important is it not to confuse them as we do whenever we use in our discussions the uncompromising language of individualisation which is proper to the second alternative, whereas what we are really pursuing in practice is the first.

There is, I fear, some amount of this sort of thing among us, a use of language much more sweeping and uncompromising than we really intend or permit to be expressed in our practice. This may be, like certain other of our inconsistent indulgences, a luxury incidental to a feeling of security. Jeshurun may be expected to kick a little when he waxes fat. No doubt, too, there have been old stupidities and repressions and meaningless artificialities that called for a strong reaction in favour of freedom. And the rise of modern biology and psychology, coinciding as it very largely did with the comfortable securities of the nineteenth century, has provided both stimulus and scientific resources for the extension of freedom. But I still ask whether the banner we set up really does stream like a thunderstorm against the wind or only appear to us to do so.

Let me quote some examples of current tendencies in

thought and expression, if not in action, which I feel ought to be fully examined in the light of all that really determines our practice before we take them as expressing what we are actually setting out to do.

There is, first of all, the extreme form of the 'unfolding' theory, the doctrine that education is nothing more than a watchful vigilance over the purely natural unfolding of potentiality. Taken in its extremer forms this doctrine seems to me to involve a refusal to take into account the necessities of civilisation, the necessity both of maintaining a civilised order and of drawing from it in specific acts of ordered *learning* under guidance the very stuff of personality itself. And the nature of the demand for specific learning, for causing the natural powers to take a specific direction and lead to the formation of a personality with specific acquirements of will and insight and skill and knowledge in terms of actuality, changes in our time with almost bewildering rapidity.

The healthy reaction in favour of giving the freest possible scope to natural powers should not involve us in such a complete concentration upon the *inward* as to neglect disastrously its effective complement in the *outward*.

I have some misgivings too about any doctrine which, while rightly emphasising inner independence and spontaneity, leads a pupil to grow up with the idea that the outer world exists solely for his service and convenience, as a reservoir from which he draws just what he feels his own personality needs, and not also as a world having its own claims upon him. The type is becoming rather common. Its opposite is the ultra-docile type which just submits all the time: people who, as Stevenson says, 'go through life like smiling images pushed from behind'. But why should we have to choose between them? 'He that is great is as he that doth serve.' The question is again one of the happy unifying of nature and art in our work, of marrying effectively independence and adaptation.

As one last instance of what seems to me unbalanced emphasis upon pure inwardness and abstract individualisation, to the neglect of concrete conditions and determinants, I might mention the sort of language that is sometimes used about teaching the pupil and not the subject. I agree, of course, that it is the pupil we teach all the time. But if we teach effectively at all, surely we must teach *something*, and that something ought to be enormously important. Important, I mean, for the pupil himself as a directing and determining of his natural powers into specific functional form. There is danger in the tendency to draw a sharp distinction between pupil and curriculum, for a well-designed curriculum is surely nothing more than our own intelligent projection of what we believe the pupil to need as means of self-fulfilment. The point is clearer if you take swimming as an example instead of Latin. What are we doing when we teach John to swim? The absurdity of asking whether it is John or swimming that we are teaching is plain enough here. Clearly, we are helping John to organise and focus his natural powers in order to achieve a new and valuable *function*. And that is precisely what we do, whatever else we teach, so far as our teaching has relevance and vitality.

So I should deprecate as, in the end, inimical to freedom any tendency to stress free individuality as being in any antagonism with the idea of a determinate curriculum. And, conversely, I should doubt whether any very definite meaning can be attached to the notion of teaching for the sake of the subject rather than for the sake of the pupil. Even in those unregenerate pre-Rousseau days when a boy could be given a text-book with the encouraging title, 'You shall make Latin whether you will or no', the ostensible reason for teaching a subject was that it was good for the pupil to know it. And pupils did learn to read and write and even speak Latin. Or are we to suppose that pupils were regarded as so many guinea-pigs to be inoculated in bacteriological fashion for the sole purpose of propagating a culture? Occasionally there may have been some idea of this sort, and the thing is not absent from our world to-day. But generally I think the difference between us and our ancestors in this regard is not that they taught the *subject*, whereas we teach the *pupil*, but that we now know a good deal more about actual teaching than they did, and are coming to a much more personalised and flexible and less tradition-ridden conception of the curriculum.

But I must hasten to a conclusion. My main theme has been that in the circumstances which we may well have to face, we shall need to re-think all our postulates of freedom, to make ourselves more precisely aware of the true nature of the freedom we are seeking, and especially to analyse thoroughly the conditions—even the limitations—within which such freedom is to be achieved.

I may be exposing myself to misunderstanding if I put the point by saying that freedom is not enough. There is a sense in which that is true and a sense in which it is not true. It is certainly true if we mean by our gospel of freedom nothing more than an attempt to give greater play to sheer spontaneity in the school, without relating such policy to the larger and highly positive implications which become clear when we analyse the whole situation. I am tempted here to quote some rather severe words of Professor Hocking, one of the wisest guides I know on this whole matter. He says: 'Freedom is a great word with which to fight oppression, but is it a word to guide the building of any positive conception of human nature? It has been so effective as a fighting tool that liberators have commonly fallen into the natural delusion that it can also, without further ado, construct an ethics. So far as they have done this, they have become the typical word-worshippers of our day, and have left the real problems of human living untouched.'

It is for this kind of reason that, of the two alternatives presented above, I am sure we shall adhere to the first even when we have made explicit all that we now take for granted, to that which might be called '*English* Freedom'. For it would seem that if freedom is to be abiding, fruitful, and serviceable to man, it must rest upon, be a function of, an agreed social discipline. Its ultimate value and significance, indeed, lie beyond that discipline, but the discipline conditions it and gives it backbone and substance, particularly in its growing stages.

On the contrary, the alternative of the more absolute type of freedom with its extreme of individualisation either leads to the social disintegration such as Löwe describes in his account of post-war Germany, and excites a reaction which makes freedom itself impossible, or passes wholly inwards and becomes a self-contained quietism that has no effect upon the world. Freedom detached from the implications of a moral order is either a riot or a desert island.

It remains now to add one or two corollaries of the position I have taken up.

In the first place, I feel that in the future we shall have to give more attention to *institutions* without giving any less attention to individuals. For it is around institutions that the battle is likely to rage. We shall need to know more about their exact modes of influence upon individuals who live in them and by them, how far they work in harmony, and how far in conflict, whether they are really what they seem to be, and how far they fail to be adequate expressions of the real needs and values of men to-day. Chief among them is still the family. But what of its future? Then there is the whole vast complex of industrial and economic institutions generally. It may require little or much examination to discover in institutions of this type inconsistencies with the kind of moral order that we wish to presuppose, and with the spirit and objects of the education that we carry on in terms of it. Their educational bearings are still largely unexplored. Most of all, we shall need to remember that the more distant goal of education in any free society is something more than the production of the appropriate type. We have succeeded as educators when we have produced personalities so well integrated within themselves, so firm in their grasp, and so unequivocal in their expression of ideal values, in a word so *free*, that they will and must react upon the institutional order that has nourished them. Otherwise, freedom is robbed both of its final fruit and its best earthly guarantee, a society that is always open at the growing end as it were, and expecting—not merely allowing—that, as individuals fulfil themselves in and through the institutional order, they will reward the service by giving of their freedom and integrity so as to bring new riches to the whole. I am not arguing here for the deliberate cultivation of young rebels, though such will always have their place. Rather the weight of the argument falls on the institutional side, to keep it reasonably plastic and open so that freedom may be justified by its fruits.

Secondly, I would call attention to the need to *universalise* our principles in the sense of applying them to all alike. I am thinking here, more particularly, of those sections of the community which the Americans describe, with a rather grim expressiveness, as 'the under-privileged'. They constitute an essential part of our problem, and it is most cheering to observe how widely the fact is coming to be appreciated. The time is coming, perhaps, when we can no longer afford, consistently with our own safety, to perpetuate in our midst what Disraeli called the Two Nations.

Then a word about the need for the cultivation among our pupils, by every possible means, of the quality of intellectual integrity. Recently, I have heard it suggested that we are rather failing to do this. It is alleged that while we are making life for our pupils both pleasant and strenuous, reaching high standards of scholarship and cultivating a healthy community life, we are failing rather in the production of persons in whom knowledge and learning have become wholly personalised, integrated, and consolidated in the unity of the whole functioning Self which knows its own groundwork, accepts responsibility for all its beliefs, and goes into life, whether critically or co-operatively, as a self-responsible and impregnable whole.

I am not able to say what truth there may be in the criticism, so I restrict myself to pointing out that it is precisely in times of far-reaching shift of anchorages that such intellectual integrity has its greatest importance. Perhaps I may add also that this matter of integrity, with its correlate of a real acceptance of responsibility, becomes important too when emphasis upon freedom in the simple sense of absence of restraint is accompanied, as it sometimes is, paradoxically enough, by a disposition to minimize the responsibility of individuals for their deliberate actions.

The mischances and deficiencies of heredity and circumstance are appealed to as affording not merely an explanation, but an excuse for moral failure, and responsibility is then spread over so wide a range of circumstances that little is left to be carried by the individual himself.

It would take most of the zest and inspiration out of our efforts for improvement of the conditions and opportunities of life generally—especially for the 'under-privileged'—if we ceased to believe that a considerable share of the responsibility for moral and personal deficiency in individuals is to be borne by society as it now is. But to over-emphasise that side of the matter so as to reduce unduly the stress on *individual* responsibility is to render our advocacy of freedom dangerously one-sided, by a dissociation of freedom from the moral and personal *stamina* which should be its fruit.

Lastly, let us look once more at the higher reaches of freedom so that we may realise, if need be, that the way of freedom is not the primrose path which some have taken it to be. Let us not romanticise childhood too much. Occasionally let us take a glance at the sternness of the demands which a real commitment to freedom may impose. Achieved freedom in the high sense of a perfected autonomy of Self, and a calm independence of circumstance is not for us all.

But we recognise it when we meet it. We do not, I think, recognise it in such utterances as the well-known one in Henley's *Invictus*:

> I am the captain of my fate,
> I am the master of my soul.

Here the forced stridency of the note bears witness to the lack of real assurance within. It is not only by whistling that we keep our courage up; recourse may also be had to shouting.

I seem rather to detect the real note in such men as Sir Thomas More and Socrates. That ironic utterance of More's on the scaffold as he pushed aside his beard while laying his head on the block: 'Pity that should be cut; that has not committed treason', seems to me the authentic voice of the really free man. He had kept the law, and now the outward loyalties could be reconciled with the personal integrity only in one way. That way the free man had to take, and his dying remark was the expression of a freedom beyond the reach of circumstance and any form of man-made law.

Much the same is true of Socrates, who was faced by the same dilemma between loyalty and personal integrity, and solved it, like More, in the only way that was open to the free man. And we remember his last words too: 'Crito, I owe a cock to Asclepius; do not forget to pay it', words that in the circumstances give us a glimpse of that same unassailable calm of the free man that we catch sight of in More's irony.

It is well, I think, when talking about freedom to recall such examples of it. Freedom at its higher levels is a noble and lovely thing, a calm and imperturbable thing. But it can also be a rather terrible and tragic thing, and it will be well both for our thinking and our practice not wholly to lose sight of that aspect of it.

EDUCATION AND VITALITY

E. Graham Howe

A TEAM of six boys from a leading public school met six boys from a naval training ship in a boxing competition. The training ship boys possessed the 'brawn'; they were tough and fought 'all out' as if they meant to win by strength alone. The public school boys possessed the 'brains'; they looked more slender and intellectual, without their opponent's robust physique and will to win. They used their heads with more skill than their hands. In the battle of 'brawn v. brains', the result in this case was in favour of the 'brawn' by four matches to two.

I mention this illustration of our problem in order to ask a question. The conflict between mind and body, head and heart, brains and brawn, is a very real one. But must we choose between the two? Or, can we combine them so that neither suffers, but both find their own advantage from association with the other? Education has a double responsibility to body and to mind, encouraging them both to finer culture and more abundant life. Can this be done, or must one always suffer at the expense of the other? Can the seeming conflict be bridged with 'and', or must the gulf between the two be widely separated by the less tolerant conjunction 'or'? To use a metaphor by which to illustrate this problem of 'incarnation', and thus ask the same question again: can Education serve both light and lantern, so that each may also serve the other in the enlightened service of the whole community? In fact, can we plan and use a method of Education that will not only *enable* life to grow, but also *encourage* it to fuller and more wholesome growth?

In the broadest and simplest terms, Life is the purpose of Education. Life more abundantly, for all and every aspect or function of the self, is our goal. But, simple as this statement may appear, nevertheless it covers infinite ignorance, because we know so little of what Life really is and means. Although it is the most intimate subject of our experience, it remains miraculous, intangible, unseen, and unknown. The little we know of it seems to die as soon as we grasp it consciously in the attempt to make it more securely our own. We can, as it were, frame life within the limits of the known, as light within lantern, but that is to lose it and not to hold it fixed. We can know all about lanterns, and that may be too much, since they can swamp the light. But it is the living spirit, the enduring flame of every human torch, which Education must nourish and encourage.

How is this to be done? The answer may first be expressed negatively: namely, not by the direct method of mechanical efficiency. We must not pursue any living objective by the direct use of power, for efficiency may promote the progress of dead things, but it will not stimulate the growth of living ones. It will hoard successfully, but it will not create. For instance, knowledge may be amassed efficiently, but not wisdom; wealth, but not health; power, but not love; material things, but not happiness. This is because knowledge, wealth, power, and all material assets are not alive and so may be caught and collected to advantage; but living things such as wisdom, love, health, and happiness must be wooed in quite another way.

If Education is to be alive, it must itself be endowed with the creative miracle of growth. This requires the intimate association of seed and soil, darkness and light, teacher and pupil, past and future, mind and body. In other words, the miracle of creation requires a certain relationship between two opposite parents, as male and female, father and mother, if the third aspect of the Trinity is to become manifest in the fact of consequence, which is the living child. No one alone can make this third, which is why the direct method must always fail as inefficient in the end. Its self-contained simplicity is too similar to the unrelated absolutism of masturbation, which is a bad habit that is inclined to breed, by imitative repetition of its own image.

The creative method evolves out of a subtler and seemingly illogical simplicity, where $1+1=3$, and $2+2=5$. In order to produce this growth or magical increase, two in relationship must woo and wed. The living formula is $A+B=C$. This is unfamiliar mathematics, because we are accustomed to the more logical statement $A+B+C = A+B+C$, but nevertheless it is the living truth. The symbolism of Life is not prose, but poetry, and its constant flow is like a river contained within banks and spanned by a bridge. Or it is the torch, the flame of which springs not from two parents only, but from four.

It is therefore necessary for Education to concern itself with parentage and relationships. If these are rightly set, the living child will grow in time. Education for life must woo through love in time, not attempting to force through power in no time. It must agree to differ and thus span the gulf between all opposites, and it must encourage a policy of circulation within the community, which is the reverse of hoarding for individual gain.

We must remember that however much we may desire to stress the importance of relationship and the value of service to the community, it is the self that counts, because it is the self that is to grow more creative and more alive in fuller integration. The self is one, in the sense that the individual is one who can say 'I am' and have a name. Each one of us, however, is also two, having two aspects related as heart and head, female and male, artist and mechanic, mystic and soldier, or impulse and conscience. From their relationship, coupled and wed, there springs the living third, the self's own 'soul' or growing point. (Note that here, as always, love is the mediator, which is the significance in daily life of the Christian ideal.)

The two opposites are neither to be confused nor identified, but to be recognised as opposite, held separate, and then grouped in the relationship of love. This applies to all related couples, both within the self and between different selves, such as in the case of teacher and taught. This is, therefore, the only way of living truly and wholly in a community, where all are to be relative and none absolute; all moving and none fixed; all included and none left out.

To carry the self's differentiation a stage further, it may be subdivided in terms of its four 'psychological functions' or 'conditions of experience'. These may be called respectively:

(1) Intuition (spiritual 'body').
(2) Thought (mental 'body').
(3) Feeling (emotional 'body').
(4) Sensation (physical 'body').

From this complex relationship, there springs the fifth, which is the living flame for which we are to seek. The term 'body' is used for each of these conditions of experience in order to make plain the fact that no one of them is in itself necessarily 'better' than any other; it is the wholeness of each and all which matters most. Each one of these 'bodies' is a part of the whole Self and is to be developed in relationship with all the others. They are equally 'real' according to their own conditions and equally worthy of 'education' in the service of the whole.

Let us set out these bodily 'garments' or levels of experience in parallel with one another and in correspondence with their own elements of the other four-part classification of fire, air, water, and earth. They then form a kind of Jacob's ladder for angels' exercise:

	ELEMENT	BODY	FUNCTION	LEVEL
I	FIRE	SPIRITUAL	INTUITION	VEST
II	AIR	MENTAL	THOUGHT	SHIRT
III	WATER	EMOTIONAL	FEELING	COAT
IV	EARTH	PHYSICAL	SENSATION	OVERCOAT

At this point we must be very sure of our direction. Firstly, the whole of this adventure must be completed as a continuous rhythmic process of evolution, without haste, delay or too presumptuous choice. Secondly, the task of life is to come down to earth in order that the kingdom of Heaven may thereon be fulfilled. It is necessary to be very clear about these points, because it is obvious that our temptation will be to stay 'in the air', where we can have the freedom of the power of thought untrammelled by the inconvenience of relationship with things as they are. On the principle that only the best is good enough for us, too often we do not come down to earth when we should. Since Heaven is better than Earth, should we not go there as fast as we can, taking our charges with us? Looking down from lofty levels, we see the best above, the worst below, so why descend? Thus Virtue turns to Vice and God to Satan, which is not His fault, but ours, for going in the wrong direction. Seeking in this way for God and what is 'good' may lead us far away from the adventure of living on earth according to His will. It seems to me that Christ made this very clear in His teaching, and it is a pity that the theologians (and indeed all our teachers) have not warned us more particularly against the dangers of seeking only for the best. Much sickness comes as a result of such partial purpose, in spite of good intentions.

Before going further, let us summarise our criticisms as to what is wrong with Education from the point of view of its creative vitality:

1. It pursues too small a purpose. It is partial instead of total in its aims and methods, seeking 'the best for a purpose' instead of 'the wholeness of life'.

2. It cuts life and people into unrelated parts and so increases conflict, both within the self and between groups. Thus it makes not peace but war.

3. Its exclusiveness cuts out other equally important ways of experience (e.g. intuition, feeling, and sensation), because

it is afraid of them, favouring in their place conscious mental processes.

4. Being so 'thoughtful', it is inclined to be 'in the air', instead of coming down to earth in practical simplicity and in adaptability to constant change of age and circumstance.

5. It is too fixed and absolute in its values, and in its ways of teaching it is repetitive rather than creative, fixing 'good' instead of growing whole. By the very nature of its good intentions, it is therefore liable to become the destroyer and enemy of Life. This is the most serious charge of the indictment.

To illustrate more clearly what I mean by the creative method, let us rearrange the four psychological functions to which I have already referred (Intuition, Thought, Feeling and Sensation) upon the form of a cross:

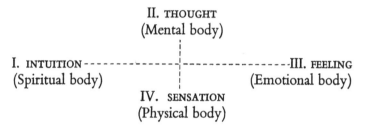

This system, however, is still static, but it can be made to live in our minds if we run an arrow from Intuition to Feeling, which will enable us to realise that it is our feelings (the arrowhead of experience) which are our growing point of impact upon the moving 'now' of time. Feelings are the touch we keep with reality, by means of sensitiveness within ourselves to every moving detail. Thus, it is the 'feeling' of life that counts, not the 'thought' of it, in spite of Descartes' dictum to the contrary.

Next, let us imagine that Thought is to act as the father and Sensation as the mother of the child Feeling, which is to be born of their union. These two, which are derived from our objective information about reality, then form the bow which sets the state of tension. Intuition and Feeling form the arrow, cross-wise, of our subjective responsiveness to such information, which has been sensitively and accurately received:

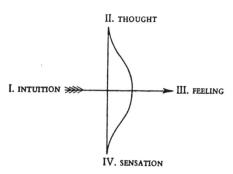

This pattern of the bow and arrow tensely strung then portrays the whole of self in creative action, sensitive, balanced, responsive, adaptable, and strong.

These four in their relationship create the fifth, which is Life, manifest with more or less abundance, in creation and experience. Our problem then becomes: how can we make this grow?

(*a*) *Purpose.* The all-round child is not to be taught in terms of progress, competitiveness, or egotistic ambition. We must learn to fail as well as to succeed, to lose as well as to gain, to feel as well as to think, which is the proof of all good sportsmanship in Life as well as in school, in work as well as in play. Our task is therefore circular and not 'up and up' in an ascending curve of progress to perfection. Only the wholeness can really be the best and no partial purpose will suffice, if our aim is Life.

(*b*) *Wholeness.* This requires a 'love-your-enemy' technique of all-inclusiveness, where nothing is to be rejected and no part of self left out. In practice, this means that all teaching is to be 'provocative', and all mistakes 'indicative', i.e. it is more important to see which way the cat jumps and why, than that it should always jump mechanically right. The aim of punishment therefore becomes corrective and creative, rather than aggressive or repressive. Like every form of teaching, it should be as 'positive' as possible, so that it can be 'positively' received.

(*c*) '*Let's see.*' Illumination is the keyword of this teacher's method. The light is to be used for seeing with, not burning by, for it is light that we require, not heat. The light also needs to be frequently directed in such a way that we can see for ourselves and illuminate our own dark places.

(*d*) *Time* must always be a law in the living process of growth, for Time is always a fact of all relationships. To be untimely is to be a bad teacher, in spite of every other virtue. It takes very little time to fertilise the seed, but growing is a much longer and more arduous process.

(*e*) *Relationships.* Things and people require to be both separated (first) and related (second). This is a double process, neither side of which can be neglected. Identification may seem convenient and virtuous, but it is false and therefore unnecessarily dangerous (e.g. imitation and hero-worship between pupil and teacher). We have to be ourselves, alone, before we can be citizens of our community. 'This is not that: but this is related to that, thus.'

(*f*) *Central Principle.* There must be some central principle, call it what you will, 'Life', 'Community', or 'God', to make the parts cohere and give meaning to the whole. This may well be the creative principle, which is 'Love', whatever that may mean. Sex (the 'facts of life' and 'biology') and Religion ('Divinity' or the Acts of St Paul) both need to be implicit in the central principle of the creative miracle which is wrought out of relationships. In the end, as in the beginning and all the time, I AM to be my SELF, while I am learning to be more all-inclusive.

(*g*) *Keep Moving.* Life is not fixed, but too often Education is; Life does not hoard (that is disease), but too often Education does; Life is circulation, and so must Education be also. Thus, questions are better than answers, and it is not enough merely to be 'right'.

(*h*) *Nourish.* This amplifies the question as to what is 'right' at any time. The derivation of Education is 'educ*are*' (to nourish) not 'educ*ere*', and leadership (i.e. dictatorship) is not enough. We need the nourishment of an adequate and balanced diet, if we are to become whole; but nourishment must be destroyed before it can be assimilated. It is no compliment to the teacher to return an undigested meal 'absolutely right' upon his desk. Therefore memory, though useful as an index of accuracy, is too suggestive of psychic constipation and can easily go too far.

(*i*) It is, of course, readily admitted that there is a place for the rubber stamp method of repetitive accuracy (e.g. learning irregular verbs). Sometimes $A + B + C = A + B + C$ and sometimes $A + B = C$, which gives rise to the question: 'Which one, when?' But the temptation in anxiety is always to stick to the first method, because it seems so safe.

The task of Education, as I see it for our time, is to teach us how to live in commonwealth in our community, which includes not any less than the brotherhood of all mankind. Our aim, therefore, is to be not less than whole, within our selves, amidst the clamouring responsibilities of all our innumerable relationships. We are to be as one, but this cannot be until our differences are all at first accepted and then united within the all-embracing circle of this common aim. Life to-day demands our service, each according to his gifts, not for ourselves alone, but for the whole community in which we live.

It is the problem of relationship which first requires solution, i.e. not you *or* me, but you *and* me; not me but us. This exceeds the practice of leader and led, teacher and pupil, for we must all eat from the same side of the heaped plate of ignorance. The day of leadership is over; there can be no new Messiah come to save us, nor is any old one of any use, unless and until we can have him dwelling within us, as creative self.

The most important fact for teachers to assimilate is the principle of duality or related opposites. Between these opposites of our two selves, or you and me, or self and circumstance, we live and move and have our being. If we are to bring Life 'down to earth', this must be our difficulty, but it is not so bad as long as we understand that it is not only 'just a job', but also a magnificent adventure. If we are in trouble, then let us hold it for a while and not be in too great a hurry for immediate solution. In the meantime we can illuminate, living sensitively and achieving a little peace within ourselves, despite the threat of War.

Life demands our toughening to endure the strain of its relationships. We are too soft; there has been too much stress upon the evils of physical masturbation and not enough realisation of the evil effect of this same false autocratic absolutism upon other planes of experience, for it can effect each one of our four bodies with increasing disaster to the living and dynamic self. We must get 'tough', yet not according to the fashion taught by war-purposive dictators. We must learn the lesson of suspense, as well as that of sensitiveness.

What is the meaning of 'endurance'? It is not that we should be hard, with grit teeth and clenched fists about our hardships, but that we should learn softly and lightly to receive our whole experience. There is a 'male' and 'female' way of our enduring, according to whether our attitude is 'hard' or 'soft', shut or open, selecting according to the preference of desire, or accepting all in free surrender to the wholeness of that which Life brings.

To-day we are faced with two alternatives, where both are wrong, and we must find that third which contains and transcends these other opposites. Let us define them:

(a) The educational system of some nations aims to make their children 'tough', because they see in absolute discipline the means to make better soldiers and victories more certain. These children are taught in terms of War and must live strenuously or be despised as weaklings. They live in a world that is 'War-minded' and are trained as efficient cannon-fodder for the engines of destruction. In spite, however, of all that they may lose of culture and independence, they do gain something from their strength and discipline, which softer schooling is inclined to lose.

(*b*) The tendency of education in our country has been to make things too easy, and we are in danger to-day of losing altogether that quality of endurance, which, through the ready acceptance of discipline, makes service to the community a stern reality. The pendulum has swung from 'You must or. .' to 'What would you like to do?' There is a degree of comradeship now between master and boy which has perhaps never been known before, and while this is certainly a great gain, it may bring about a loss of this quality of endurance which also has its value.

(*c*) The keyword for our understanding of this 'transcendent third', to ensure that it contains the best of those other two, is (as it always must be) 'Love'. If love is true, its truth is something that endures.

This quality of endurance is a deeper discipline than that which War demands, for it is not aiming at any partial purpose, such as victory in battle, but at a state of wholeness which knows no goal nor ending. Endurance of this kind must take all hardship softly, with open heart and accurate sensitiveness, undefended, all-embracing, patient, and mature. It is like an open flower that does not close its petals to the storm; or an open cup, into which all experience is allowed to fall, so that its bitterness as well as sweetness may be consumed in our full experience of life.

Strangely enough, this is the woman's way of all-enduring unconditional love. But also, in practice, it is the way of all great adventure. The mountain climber, the explorer, and the athlete all know the advantage of being relaxed about a state of strain, of being satisfied in spite of all they lack, and of being content even with their discontent. This ability to live amongst the great adventurers and explorers of body and mind is something which we must not lose in easy idleness, for there are more demands upon our 'fitness' to-day than perhaps have ever been before. Education must teach us wholly to live and gladly to endure.

INTERNATIONAL EDUCATION

G. H. Sauerwein

VOLTAIRE's well-known words will be no doubt familiar to you all: 'If we are to have a discussion, let us first define what we mean.' This alone can lead to a fruitful and scientific exchange of thoughts. The subject which we have under discussion requires, more than any other, a precise and deliberate outline.

We live in troubled times; one of the main troubles is the uncertainty and lack of definition of many of the notions which are put up for universal discussion. Foremost amongst these ideas is that of International Education. Those who like ourselves defend and propagate the idea of international education, lay ourselves open to criticism as dreamers, enemies of tradition, citizens of cosmopolis—in a word we are accused of belittling such notions as nationalism, and the narrower implications of country and people.

There could be no greater injustice. We remain unaffected by such attacks since we ourselves attack the narrow utilitarianism which according to the old saying, 'ubi bene ibi patria', stands for personal welfare as a criterion for membership of a community. Our condemnation extends to the colourless cosmopolitan, who is a true chameleon, everywhere in apparent harmony with his surroundings, and yet nowhere at home. We also strongly object to the sentimental indulgence in brotherly love for all mankind, which gushes over the brotherhood of nations and races and forgets the natural bonds which exist between fellow-countrymen and the duties they entail.

We realise that a state is not merely a utilitarian union but a higher form of community, based on a cultural inheritance. Each of us is rooted in the soil of family, land, and nation. From this soil we draw our life-energy. National education can only thrive on the nourishment afforded by the consciousness and manifestation of its linguistic, cultural, and social characteristics.

International education, as I understand it, can never be the negation of national education; it is its complement and its confirmation. We aim at no narrow segregation: rather are we open to any external suggestion. International education means that we should seek the understanding of foreign languages and peculiarities through a profound realisation of our own values and historical development. Emphasis on national individuality and special formation should not hinder closer communion with foreign nations. We are bound to recognise the perpetual interflow of international currents in the spiritual and economic planes.

Such an interflow is rational and natural, and I feel sure that you in England realise its potentialities. The intellectual and economic structure of your vast Empire demands it: since that Empire is, in fact, an outstanding proof and example of such an interflow of forces. The British Empire spreads over the whole earth: it embraces a variety of people, languages, and cultures, and binds them into a single political unit. It develops in Englishmen a sense of world citizenship and tolerance, which has made them the greatest colonising people in the world. The strength of England is drawn from East and West. Orient and Occident have amalgamated in your Empire, and this amalgamation is the source of your superiority.

The British Empire does not derive its greatness from mere size, it is not a homogeneous country, but the result of the fusion and interpenetration of the opposing forces of its various parts. For generations East and West have influenced each other. Exchange is a fundamental law: it is an intellectual law. Exchange means motion. Segregation means death. Within the Empire individual views and faiths are respected. While anarchy is not encouraged, since it is the enemy of liberty, personality is given full scope for development. This freedom gave birth to that modern knight—the gentleman.

Political leadership in England represents ideal gentleman-hood. Leaders must have a profound knowledge of human psychology. They must have psychological tact. The Empire could never have been built otherwise. Nowhere are these qualities more apparent than in the recognition of religious and cultural freedom and the utilisation of such emotions as the driving force behind the Empire. MacDougal, the English psychologist, rightly asserts in his *Fundamentals of Social Psychology* that the English are always conscious of the limits within which they can exert their strength. Their action has therefore never been destructive, but has always created new centres of influence. How can one otherwise explain the fact that so vast an Empire can be kept together with so little effort?

A practical knowledge of foreign languages and an insight into the psychology of foreign people is a vital necessity for a world-embracing democracy.

And now, as a contrast to the vast dominions of your Empire stands a very small country, Switzerland, which is so situated at the very heart of Europe as to be the point of intersection of European cultural influences. It has long been recognised in Switzerland that intellectual and economic exchanges are of vital importance. Consequently, this country has been for ages the nursery of international culture. Most foreigners are unable to understand the characteristics of this tiny political unit. Just as its natural characteristics in the north and in the south, in mountain and plain, have influenced each other, so have its three cultural currents been united into one stream, by historical necessity.

Its people have four national languages and yet feel that they belong together, bound by the thought of Swiss independence, liberty, and solidarity. We Swiss fully recognise what we owe to German, French, and Italian culture, but our intellectual individuality is nevertheless unimpaired, and is the result of the fusion of various nationalities. This attitude makes the Swiss free in his decisions, free from racial conceit, and free from the arrogance of rank. Our great political economist Professor Dr Max Huber has expressed this clearly, when he points out that that state is reasonable which is built not on the idea of exclusive nationality, but on the free combination of its component parts.

The free union of nationalities and cultures tends towards the predominance of the intellect and therefore raises human relations to a higher plane. The more nations isolate themselves from the others, the more does Switzerland fight to maintain the ideals of humanity by setting an example and by its effort for international understanding.

In spite of a growing necessity for mutual understanding and co-operation on economic, cultural, and political planes, the tendency towards national isolation is ever stronger. The longer this tendency lasts, the less will people be inclined to understand the virtues and qualities of foreign people. Contrasts and opposition are flourishing and culminate in armaments. Foreign relations are increasingly overshadowed by the influence of autocracies. International law is losing more and more of its importance and influence.

One of the leaders of international understanding says: 'If we consider Europe to be one great intellectual organism, we can but recognise that this organism is suffering from a deep spiritual depression at the present time. All, or nearly all, nations show the same symptoms of irritability and moral fatigue; they show a lack of optimism, an ever-present suspicion and distrust, a typical nervousness and restlessness which are the result of general uncertainty. This mutual distrust is daily proved to be stronger than mutual confidence. The whole of Europe is under the influence of this unhealthy atmosphere, which is fatal to free and happy intercourse. It is oppressive and paralysing.'

This deplorable condition of uncertainty, distrust, and mutual hostility is bitterly felt by all intellectual people in the whole of Europe. We have a double problem to face: to remove both the spiritual and the economic depressions on the Continent.

An extremely intelligent and well-known woman, Mme Curie, has said: 'Let us fight for an international culture, which will respect national culture; for personality and talent; for the domination of science; for moral disarmament and for peace.' Madame Curie fought those battles without any hope of immediate success. In 1929, she wrote to her daughter: 'I think that international work is painful and tiring, but it is absolutely necessary to go on with it, however great the efforts and sacrifices may be.'

It is not difficult to explain the necessity for international understanding to intelligent and sensible people. The difficulty begins with realisation. Defensive action against those forces which are a danger to humanity should be successful, so long as we do not waste our energy on the past, but show an interest in new ideas and look to those who are still at a formative age: the youth of the country. International understanding amongst adults must lead to an international education of youth. We must do our best to prevent the rising generation from being contaminated by the prevailing mentality of hatred. 'Whoever holds youth holds the future', is the war-cry of the different camps. We would rather say more modestly: 'Whoever holds youth holds responsibility.' It is not enough to arrange conferences, to speak continuously of good-will and to appeal to men's common sense. In the first place we must have practical action and untiring work, in order to educate the younger generation to that knowledge and consciousness of the world which will enable it to solve the problems of the future.

The building-up of the new generation naturally begins as soon as the child begins to think, i.e. in that hour of its life when it becomes aware of reality, and its mind is opened to external influences. A great modern poet once said: 'all will be right, if the youth of Europe receive an education on the same principles in every country.' Youth alone has no set principles and has no rooted prejudices; the young generation is entirely open to anything new and eminently capable of understanding foreign characteristics. It is responsive to foreign impressions, and its intuitions and instincts are sound. At this emotional age, friendships and relations between members of various nations may be realised, and it is not unlikely that such a youthful friendship may lead, later on, to economic and political consequences of great importance.

The question now arises: how are we to bring young people of various countries together? For only education in an international community can lead to success. Other proposals, based on a modification of the syllabus of instruction in various countries might be of some assistance, but on the whole they are insufficient and problematic.

With this aim in view, well-meant advice is given in many congresses, and particularly in Geneva, that history should be taught in a neutral way to avoid any direct criticism which might arouse ill-feeling. However, we are convinced that the political and military history of any country must always be influenced by national considerations, judgments, and valuations. It will always be very difficult to be impartial and without bias.

A more promising proposal is to develop the *history of culture* side by side with political and military history. Whereas the latter two forms invariably arouse hatred and bitterness, cultural history shows evidence of the interchange of thought and influence, of great discoveries and achievements. As far as military history is concerned, nations are considered solely as enemies. But cultural history shows them as brethren who understand how it is possible for one country to fecundate another; how one discovery completes another; how the welfare of one nation can improve social conditions in neighbouring ones. But it is not sufficient to teach cultural history as something which belongs only to the past, and a further essential requirement for an effective pacification would be to afford the youth of Europe a chance of *living* cultural history. Books and schools are only part of man's education; the most essential things he must always learn through his sense of observation.

The most effective method for us would thus be to bring the youth of different countries not only into superficial contact, but also into a community capable of promoting creative work and real friendship. The question cannot be completely solved, however, unless we succeed in finding a form which both safeguards national characteristics and ensures a free exchange of international values. Our formula would thus be: *National education in an international school.*

You may at first think that this is all a dream; though, after all, rather a fine one. Can such an idea be realised? I hope that I have proved that national and international education can, in our opinion, be well combined, that they need not be *contradictio in adjecto.* I know I am addressing practical and experienced people. You have no use for mere theory. You surely believe in the principle of Goethe: 'Only that which is fertile can be true.' You will always mistrust mere theories so long as these have not been proved by experiment, have not passed from the abstract to the concrete, from dream to reality.

I shall therefore venture to call your attention to a practical experiment due to the founder of Montana College, Dr Max Husmann, and to explain shortly its most outstanding points. No tendency to boast, no misplaced vanity, induce me as his collaborator to put these facts before you, but only the strong desire to propagate our ideas and to prove, through this practical example, that they can be realised.

'Ideas are meant to be realised.' This is the motto of the founder of the International School at Montana on the Zugerberg. Looking back into the past, Dr Husmann says: 'I visualised a school, a modern centre of education for future generations belonging to various nations. Present-day exigencies should be satisfied by such a school: true practical knowledge, obtained through individual schooling; workshops will be built, play-grounds fit for the needs of modern youth will be provided for physical development. Above all a college will be built in the sunny mountains of central Switzerland, in a healthy situation amidst meadows and pinewoods. Away from the nerve-racking atmosphere of big cities, children will develop in the sunlight. For many years it was all a dream. But at times dreams become real, if faith stands behind them. What is the good of calculating and planning without that faith? I believed in the idea, and this gave me strength.'

Chance or fate? At any rate he found the place he dreamed of; a flat alpine plateau, easily accessible and yet sufficiently removed from towns, in quiet and reposeful surroundings, a piece of Swiss ground about which a poet once said that it was the quintessence of the fairylike beauty of the country, a place which must induce happiness in those who dwelt there.

So the work could begin. In its vast surroundings the new school grew up. Sunny classrooms, gymnasiums, workshops, fives and tennis courts, football grounds, swimming pool and shady open-air classes for the summer school, all contributed towards the first requirement of modern education: health.

Present times make a heavy call on our organism. Man, however, tries to protect himself against decay; the new conditions have bred a longing for healthy physical culture. It was natural and necessary that our youth should be educated in the mountains, which had done so much to cure the sick. Prevention is better and easier than cure. Let us, therefore, protect youth, let us give it conditions of life in which it may be strengthened, let us just give those who are not necessarily bound to great towns the right to enjoy the advantages of healthy surroundings.

We must further remember that this place lies in Switzerland, a country which has already proved its suitability for scholastic activities over centuries, owing to the happy combination of many factors: healthy climate and location, the centre of Latin and Germanic culture, and above all a long tradition and a series of outstanding personalities, who were far sighted enough to take in new ideas, and who yet were practical and experienced enough to preserve something of the good old methods. Switzerland stood aloof from many factors which, especially after the great war, influenced the mental development of many a country. Switzerland also escaped the danger of condemning anything which was traditional and believing only in the extreme ideas of modern times. Before the war the *auctoritas patriae* and blind obedience were the basis of education. After the war it was in some countries condemned, hated, and abolished, and replaced by absolute freedom, which only too often led to anarchy and revolution.

We have tried to combine the best of old approved methods with new educational principles and achievements, and we hope in this way to form the type of man needed at the present time. Such a man should be physically and mentally fit, with unspoilt characteristics, with resistance and self-control, equipped with a clear knowledge and an open mind to meet the social requirements of our days.

Our aim is to transplant the town child into the healthy mountains, where he may indulge in daily sports of undoubted educational value, and to develop a system of education which allows maximum individual development of personality. But all this is of course only a necessary and obvious preliminary. The essential and peculiar side of our school is that the boys who are brought up under these conditions and according to those principles are members of *different* nationalities, divided into groups of approximately equal size.

Here you see the essence of national education in an international milieu. On one side you have a close and fruitful contact between different nationalities in communal daily life, during games and work; on the other side, you avoid the danger of flat cosmopolitanism. The boy must not lose contact with his own culture: close contact with the home school must be kept up.

This particular requirement has been entirely neglected till now in international schools, and yet it has become more and more important, owing to the development of European culture during the last decade. A satisfactory solution can only be found if both these requirements are fulfilled.

If this is not the case, the results of an international school will never be good. It can never achieve its proper aims, since no true national groups exist as characteristic entities which can get into touch with each other. They would rather be replaced by heterogeneous groups, which leave everything to chance, and will, after a short time, lose their national characteristics, lose contact with their own culture and home, and favour the type of internationalism which creates that type of man who is at home everywhere and nowhere. Such schools are only schools for languages, though they may impart a certain amount of general knowledge, and their temporary success depends on the personality of their headmaster.

Please do not misunderstand us; we know how suitable Switzerland is for educational purposes, but we absolutely refuse to drive foreigners into a form of life entirely different from their national one. A young man is not a mere field for experiment, with new methods—and how often are those methods only a passing mode, the fruit of individual fantasy! However important the individual and his ideas may be, they are only fruitful and helpful if they are of real interest to the majority. One of the most important experts on educational matters was Heinrich Pestalozzi. He said: 'A human being must be able to help himself in the world; our task is to teach him how to do so.' School and life, education and reality, must be in correct proportion.

The most important question for parents is the future of their children. To-day, the answer is more difficult than ever, owing to the general uncertainty. It is no longer possible to rely upon one's own resources and financial means to secure a child's career. No father, however rich he may be at present, feels absolutely sure that he will be able, when the time comes, to give his child a proper start in life. In your country, also, the financial situation of the upper classes has been weakened. The only real assets are: a good general education and a strong personality. Whatever the world may be to-morrow, mentally, socially, and economically, it will always need healthy, tactful, and efficient men, able to fill key positions; but education must be such as to widen the outlook, teach foreign languages, and impart a deeper knowledge of foreign nations and culture, while insisting at the same time on national values.

Now the question is, is it possible to meet these requirements without boys losing valuable time, and without weakening their national contacts and relations?

The aim of Montana College is to undertake this task. But for this purpose, a problem of extraordinary difficulty had first to be solved: the official recognition of the various national sections by their respective countries and governments. Students have always attended foreign universities and colleges, but they generally had to pay for the linguistic and moral advantages of their stay abroad, with a serious loss of time, since the period of their stay abroad could not be accepted as part of their official studies by the home authorities. Thus many a young student, who would have liked to go abroad and to get into closer touch with foreign people, languages, and culture, found it impossible to do so without seriously affecting his chances of success at home. Lost time cannot easily be made up, owing to the increasing demands of the curriculum and the necessity for earning a living at an early stage.

Your country helped us by giving the members of the English Section the right to sit for the School Certificate in the school itself. Similar concessions had to be obtained from other countries, and this was particularly difficult in the case of the more autocratic states. But nothing is impossible. 'Why should not', said Dr Husmann to himself, 'reasonable and sensible leaders be won over to a sensible idea? What cannot be achieved by correspondence and petitions can perhaps be achieved by the effect of personal contact, faith, and conviction, and perhaps, that spark of enthusiasm might fire the other side.' In spite of criticism and doubt, he found his way into the presence of leading political personalities; he spoke to Barthou, one time foreign minister of France, and even stood before Mussolini—and the day came when even Italy recognised the justice and necessity of his idea, and established a section of its own at Montana College. Italy was followed by Austria, Switzerland, and Holland, all of which formed official national sections and conceded the right to hold official examinations on the School premises.

The Zugerberg is now not only a mountain dedicated to youth, but also a league of nations, in the best sense perhaps.

The expression 'official section' may be explained more fully. It is a community of boys from the same country, who naturally wish to follow their own special form of national education. They are under the personal control of a master from their own country and are instructed in their own subjects by masters of their nationality. They are thus taught the value of their own history and language under the best conditions, they have their club, their newspapers and books from home, and are thus not isolated in a strange country, but always surrounded by the homely atmosphere of national tradition.

But they are free to invite members of other sections and nations as guests to their regular club meetings, and thus they become pleasantly familiar with the characteristics of these foreigners. The dining hall affords further occasions for intercourse, and so do games and sports, so that the boys cannot help getting into close touch with the representatives of various nationalities; they form friendships with their foreign

comrades and thus enjoy to the fullest degree the potentialities of national and international education. The study
and practice of foreign languages is, therefore, extremely
important for the school. It is both a tragedy and a comedy
in our days that, in spite of technical achievement and
travelling facilities, we are still so clumsy when it comes to
making ourselves understood. A few helpless sentences about
the weather, some faint remembrance of a few grammatical
rules, and one may perhaps get over tea or lunch with a foreign
guest; but sensible and intelligent conversation is impossible,
and yet it is perhaps the first and last chance of deeper understanding and closer contact. Let us admit freely that the few
lessons in languages of our school days scarcely enable us to
read a foreign book, and certainly never lead us to a complete
mastery of the foreign idiom. This is entirely different in an
international school, where the learner's ear adapts itself to
the finest differentiations of the foreign language by daily
conversation, and where, above all, the student daily realises
the absolute necessity of mastering languages, and can put
to daily practical use that which he has already learnt.

Our organisation is such that a perfect knowledge of foreign
languages really results. This method not only includes the
teaching of grammar and syntax by masters, whose mother-
tongue the language is, but also enables the boy to take up the
study of many subjects in a foreign language, an educational
medium which is improved by daily contact with boys of
different nationalities. There is nothing extraordinary therefore in finding boys of thirteen or fourteen years of age, who
already speak two, three, or even four languages absolutely
fluently, and who act in plays with boys of other nationalities;
in fact, you would find it hard to pick out the foreign boys
by their accent.

'Wessen das Herz voll, des geht der Mund über'—out of
a full heart the mouth speaketh! So I could tell you much more
about education, internationalism, about captains and prefects,
about our English house system, but I am afraid that I have

already taken up too much of your time and attention, and I will therefore close with hearty thanks to the English nation, which in its public-school system has given us the best example of a perfect schooling of will and character. Your aims may differ from ours in many ways, but we too try to guard ourselves against any form of over-estimation of the intellect. We try to find a living synthesis of will and knowledge, so as to form that type of man who later on in life proves himself a personality in private and public life. Our aim is only reached if our school is able to produce an *élite*, who speak foreign languages thoroughly, who know foreign customs and manners from experience, and who are able to get along with anyone. We are convinced that such an *élite* must be an advantage to any country, as statesmen, or in the universities, industry, or commerce. They have those natural bonds of comradeship, education, and sympathy with other countries, which they have acquired in their youth. Perhaps it may be possible that from this group of friendly people in each country a better attitude may arise and spread. Perhaps it may lead to an altogether better future understanding between European nations, and if Montana College, in a modest way, can have contributed to the pacification of our old Continent through the realisation of national education in an international school, we should be only too proud of our contribution to the world.

CURRICULUM REFORM

W. D. Johnston

IT is one of the difficulties of much that is said or written on education that it must be so entirely a matter of opinion, and to talk at large on a big subject in a short time inevitably commits the speaker to sweeping statements which, were the time available, would be qualified or at any rate supported by evidence. If, then, I seem to make wide assumptions, and appear too often to be irritatingly dogmatic, I may be forgiven.

One other point: I am not entitled to represent anyone but myself. I speak entirely as a private member of the Association of Preparatory Schoolmasters, and would commit no one else to my views. There is, however, a fairly large group of Preparatory Schoolmasters who believe that there is urgent need of a revolutionary change in our curriculum and teaching practice, and this is my excuse for using frequently the first person plural, instead of the first person singular.

To plunge then *in medias res*, we believe that schools often dull and blunt the curiosity and enthusiasm of the boy: that they find him mentally alert, eager, and adventurous, and too often leave him bored, listless, and incurious.

This was well put some years ago by Mr Malim, the former Master of Wellington, when speaking to Preparatory Schoolmasters on this subject.

'There is', he said, 'plenty of active curiosity at this age. There is, at any rate, no unwillingness to ask questions. But when you and we have finished with these eager children, some of them have become completely devoid of any desire to learn or understand.'

Considering the class from which we draw our boys, and

the advantages of upbringing, environment and education with which they start, we do not seem to turn out anything like as high grade an article as we should. Given great qualities of character—courtesy, courage, unselfishness, generosity, sense of justice, and fair dealing—our boys still lack attributes which in the nature of things they should acquire, and which two generations ago were accepted as the mark of an educated man. Particularly in post-war years— partly no doubt because they are post-war years, but persisting in an unaccountable way—there does seem to be, among young people, an ignorance of, and a distaste for the things of the mind—books, pictures, music—an absence of a sense of values, and often a deliberate cult of low-browism, which is disturbing. We are living in a vulgarised world, and yet this lack of dignity and good taste—to put it no higher—is coincident with an enormous increase in the number of boys passing through Preparatory and Public Schools as compared with fifty years ago.

And when, in the light of this criticism, we come to look at the curriculum, it does seem that we have sacrificed thoroughness to expediency and allowed concretions of information with high-sounding labels to be foisted on us as obligatory subjects without any attempt to relate them to the educational whole. The result is an irrational and unsuitable curriculum. Far too many subjects are taught, and they are unrelated, so that the curriculum is without unity or purpose. It is remote from a boy's life and interests and therefore beyond his comprehension. Emphasis is too heavily placed on factual knowledge for its own sake. There is little effort, because of lack of time, to teach a boy method, or to train him how to find out things for himself. The curriculum is designed for the scholar, and the interests of the ordinary boy are neglected.

A few weeks ago there appeared in *The Sunday Times* an article on 'Educational Heresies' by Dr Alington, formerly Headmaster of Eton. I should like to have time to read you that article in full, for it covers, almost exactly, and far better than I could, the ground I wish to cover this afternoon. A short extract, however, must suffice.

'The first educational heresy', he says, '—a comparatively modern one—is that an educated man ought to know something about everything. The old belief was much sounder: it laid down that a well-educated man knew everything about something. Its reverse is particularly dangerous nowadays when the field of possible knowledge has been so enormously enlarged that there is only time for the merest smattering of the subjects to be acquired.'

This trouble has been actually exaggerated by the increased efficiency of the teaching machine and by the enormously increased importance attached everywhere, and especially in the business world, to examinations which from being our servants are now in a fair way to become our masters. Those of us who believe in reform repudiate the idea that five credits in the School Certificate Examination is a worthy aim for any educational system. For the ordinary boy to be really creditably informed in so great a mass of organised knowledge is a stark impossibility: in consequence, the credit standard has to be set so miserably low that as the culminating point in a boy's education it is a frank absurdity. And it has for a large and increasing number of boys become the culminating point.

Now to return to the Preparatory schoolboy.

Let us consider for a moment the plight of a little boy of eight entering his Preparatory School. He can talk, and often talk surprisingly well, from a limited vocabulary on subjects which interest him. He can, perhaps, read tolerably well and he can write, if he is given a great deal of time, with some fluency. He is ripe for training in his own language, for introduction to the natural world around him, for all kinds of direct experience in making and doing, in experiment and adventure; and all these things can be correlated and given direction and meaning if training in Speech,

Reading, and Writing is made the end in view. In two or three years we could teach him an enormous amount of interesting and useful facts about the real world, not as an end in itself, but merely as a by-product in teaching him *how* to work. We could teach him how to find out what he wants to know, how to arrange his facts so that they will be most efficient and useful to him, how to express in worthy language the thousands of exciting impressions that he is getting, or ought to be getting, from the material world around him, and above all we could introduce him to the delight of reading and the joy of expression.

But athwart the path of this natural development there are soon to be thrown shadows—Latin grammar, French, the whole of English History, the whole of World Geography, and other similar monstrosities. The impossibility in the time available of treating these enormous entities adequately or in a way that will arouse any real interest, beyond the evanescent interest and romance with which the little boy is pathetically eager to invest anything new, is soon obvious. But if he is ever to pass an examination, certain concretions of information bearing these labels must be built up in his mind, and so we fall back on outlines of the subjects to be taught. Now an outline of a big body of organised information may be an excellent thing, but except for the expert it is almost meaningless, and for the immature and untrained mind quite useless.

History, perhaps, supplies the most devastating example of this kind of thing. We take a text-book of English History of possibly 600 pages (although one of such a length would be unusually large and detailed) on which we are going to work. Now I say, without fear of contradiction, that to attempt to compress into such a space an outline of the whole of English History is to perpetrate a series of half-truths and misstatements, if not downright falsehoods, that makes such a book a positive menace to anyone who has not had a thorough historical training. But we have only two periods a week for English History: there is no time for any method other than the lecture method—the most useless and inefficient for this stage and subject. And so we take this mass of second hand (or more often third or fourth hand) information, arbitrary judgments, and subjective decisions, and pump it into the child as truth. If he is a clever boy and remembers some of it, it does irreparable harm to his critical faculties. The majority being entirely untrained to work over and organise such a mass of information get into a complete muddle, and the result, although quite worthless, is historically harmless.

The result of the failure to understand, and the cramming of a jumbled mass of inaccurate facts into the boy's mind, are, however, far from harmless. A further blow is given to his already rapidly waning self-confidence, and the thought begins to be born in his mind that he is not very clever and will not ever be much good at books.

And the same kind of criticism could be applied, *mutatis mutandis*, to other subjects.

This seems to me to be the really damaging thing about our present system. Many boys who, treated differently, might have become masters of some small part of human knowledge and who at any rate are capable of mastering their own language, are thus permanently discouraged from continuing any form of literary work as soon as the compulsion of their school days is removed. They accept, with pathetic humility, the judgment that, because they have failed at achievements which for lack of preparation are entirely beyond their powers, they are half-wits and illiterates.

Now this frustration, and sense of failure, against which we are protesting, comes still more, we believe, from the custom which survives from the days of an earlier and less crowded curriculum, of starting little boys on the study of two foreign languages at an age when their knowledge of their own is entirely rudimentary, and in particular to the enormous amount of time given to Latin at an immature stage. We are unanimous as to the value of classical studies. We feel that they must always form part of a true liberal education. But we believe that in the early stages they should be approached through English and that for some boys, though perhaps not even for the majority, English will be the only medium through which the value of the classics as an instrument of education will ever be possible. We believe that a later start in Latin, after a real linguistic discipline in English has been achieved, will produce many more classical scholars, and that, even in the shorter time available, boys will cover more ground and will cover it more effectually than they do at present.

We want, then, to make all that a boy learns subordinate to a thorough training in Speech, Reading, and Writing, which we conceive to be the true aim of a boy's literary education at his Preparatory School. 'English is not merely the medium of our thought, it is the very stuff and process of it. It is itself the English mind, the element in which we live and work.' It is, therefore, the boy's chief means of understanding the world around him, of acquiring knowledge and of expressing himself. We wish English to be the spine of the curriculum and other subjects to be admitted in order of merit, as time can be found for them. We would use Poetry and English Literature primarily for the boy's delight and also to train his critical faculties and sense of form. We would use History and Geography—not in outline, but by taking units of these subjects which can be most easily related to a boy's life and studying them intensively, less with an idea of amassing facts than with the idea of training him how to approach historical and geographical matter. Obviously, local history and local geography, where the boy can touch and see as well as read and listen, would be our starting-point here. In the same way we would use the arts, nature study, and handcraft of all kinds, primarily as servants of the end we have in view, i.e. training in Speech, Reading, and Writing, and secondarily for their own content and value in relating the boy to the world he lives in.

We believe that for the little boy 'Knowledge that is to remain a permanent possession must at the beginning be gained through direct contact with material objects and through the actual experience of the senses. It must consist of something experienced and something done: and all subsequent knowledge, if it is to be effective and lasting, must have in it this element of actual experience and achievement even when gained at second hand.' In short, we want to start with what a boy knows when he comes to us and stretch out his mind from and through what he knows to what he doesn't.

PHYSICAL EDUCATION IN THE CURRICULUM

Gerald W. Murray

I ASSUME that my task is to state what Physical Education really means, and how it can be introduced into the curriculum of boys' schools to-day. But I do not propose to define Physical Education, for, though there are many definitions current, most of them are unsatisfactory and some of them misleading. I should prefer to describe a department of Physical Education as it might work in a modern school.

In its widest interpretation Physical Education embraces all the physical activities in which boys take part, together with periodic weighing and measuring, and examinations of physique. It includes some study of change in normal and abnormal growth and development, and it should work in close connexion with the school doctor. In addition, it is essential that there should be a strong link with the academic side of education, and it requires the friendly co-operation of the headmaster, housemasters, and all others with whom the boys come into contact.

Such an ideal is comprehensive and perhaps somewhat ambitious; for the moment we may confine ourselves to those parts of Physical Education with which the department is more directly concerned; that is gymnastics and the games or sports which are usually classed as minor sports at public schools, the collection of statistics of physique, and so on.

In pure gymnastics the work may be divided conveniently into three groups; educational, recreational, and voluntary work. Educational gymnastics is the foundation on which all else is built. It aims at developing normal mobility, strength, and agility. Overstrain and any tendency to acrobatics should be avoided. Every effort should be made to create good physical habits, such as correct posture, carriage, breathing, sitting, walking, and running. Once acquired these habits remain for life. As Sir George Newman has said: 'If there be a test of the strength, tone, and balance of the body, it is posture. Good posture indicates health and soundness, bad posture the reverse.'

Perhaps I should attempt to explain the difference between the words posture and carriage as employed by physical educationists. Though one word is often used to express the meaning of both, I think that posture means the position of the body when at rest, and carriage the position of the body when in motion. For example, good posture would be the correct positioning of the body in the standing or sitting position, good carriage the correct alignment of the body when walking or running. Classroom conditions are often such that a boy must spend a great part of his time in bad positions. The sitting position can be a menace to good posture. Poor lighting, old and unsatisfactory desks, or backless benches are all contributory factors. It might be thought that most people walk and run and sit properly by nature; but this is not so, and a large part of the work of educational gymnastics consists in correcting bad habits which may have been formed, and in inculcating good habits. Muscle is an elastic substance and tends to acquire a habit length. By means of appropriate exercises muscles are lengthened or shortened until the right balance is attained between opposing groups, and good tone of the whole muscular system assured. But it is of little value to teach correct movements in the gymnasium, if boys revert to poor carriage outside. Moreover, conscious efforts to hold the body erect quickly induce fatigue. Nevertheless, it is possible to so train boys that the maintenance of good carriage and posture become automatic and completely separated from conscious thought. In addition, we strive to retain the natural mobility of joints and the maximum power of contraction of muscle with which boys are normally endowed. We aim at developing the physical powers of each individual to the highest point of which he is capable. We also teach relaxation and selective muscle-control, which, with the good postural reflexes inculcated in the minds of the boys, enables them to fulfil the functions of their daily lives with the minimum expenditure of nervous and muscular energy.

The syllabus used to secure these desirable ends is based on a mixture of Swedish and Danish work which has been adapted to fit the needs of English schools. Particulars of this will be found in the *Board of Education Syllabus of Physical Training*, 1933; *A Reference Book of Gymnastic Training for Boys*, 1927, now in process of revision; and *A Handbook of Recreation and Physical Fitness for Youths and Men*, 1937.

In recreational gymnastics we attempt to apply the mobility, strength, control, agility, relaxation, rhythm, and co-ordination attained during the educational periods to the various sports and games. Boys are often slow off the mark, and some are unable to apply those qualities acquired in the gymnasium to increase their general aptitude, speed, and alertness. If this applied training be purposeful, much improvement can be obtained.

Voluntary gymnastics may be said to have three objects. Firstly, to improve the standard of those who are interested in gymnastics as a recreation; secondly, to give an opportunity to proficient gymnasts to enjoy advanced work in vaulting, in agility, and on fixed apparatus; thirdly, to help by special classes those who have fallen behind the normal standards through illness or accident, on account of poor physique, or from lack of natural aptitude.

Apart from gymnastics, it seems natural that the department of Physical Education should control most, if not all, of the activities which are normally classed as minor sports. The movements required in these sports are more closely allied to gymnastics, and many of them may be taught in classes inside or outside the gymnasium itself. Athletics, Swimming, Boxing, and Fencing are obvious examples. In the summer a lesson might well start with some free-standing movements and proceed to the teaching of the fundamentals of athletics or swimming by class work or in groups; for, if these sports are connected directly with the department, the Director becomes responsible, and so better teaching and coaching is available for every boy in the school than when these sports are left to fill up odd moments of a boy's spare time.

In order to ensure that full benefit is derived from Physical Education, it is essential that sufficient time should be devoted to the subject of educational gymnastics. The Board suggests a minimum of two $\frac{3}{4}$-hour periods a week for seniors and three such periods for juniors, with additional time for recreational training and voluntary work. It is important that the periods allotted to educational gymnastics should be taken in school hours, for the work is really educational and, as such, should not have to compete against games for popularity. The work must be continued throughout the school and not dropped in the Certificate forms or in the Sixths, where indeed it is often most needed. It is perhaps not likely that many schools will give so much time to gymnastics; and work of some value can be done, if there be allocated two morning periods a week for junior forms and one for the seniors, provided that some further time is given to recreational work and that facilities for voluntary classes exist.

In addition to arranging a time-table, it is also necessary to provide a sufficient number of people to supervise the work. In my opinion, it is absolutely essential that the man at the head of the department should be a schoolmaster of University standing and therefore on terms of equality with other members of the teaching staff. In addition to a thorough training in all the branches of his specialised work, he should have a good knowledge of academic subjects and a sympathetic understanding of the problems of his colleagues. He must be a good organiser, able to maintain an easy discipline without formality, and so approachable that at least the majority of the boys can talk to him with confidence. It will be an advantage if he continues to teach some subjects not connected with Physical Education, for this will facilitate co-operation with his fellow masters and form a closer link between the academic subjects and Physical Education in the minds of the boys. In other words the gymnasium will cease to be 'a thing apart' and come to be recognised as an essential factor in every school.

I do not believe that a young man fresh from the University and the Training College is suitable for the position of Director in a large school. I think that such a man should spend several years as an assistant to a Director in another school, where he can learn to overcome the difficulties of the classroom, the gymnasium, and the playing fields. When he becomes a Director, he will need the position and dignity usually accorded to senior masters; and he must be so far free from the faults of youth and inexperience as to fill adequately such a position.

However, the Director could not possibly run the department alone. There must be further assistance. Undoubtedly, the best way to organise a department of Physical Education is to have a team of interested masters led unobtrusively by the Director, and many assistant masters could give valuable help in taking gymnastics classes. At present, few masters are sufficiently trained for the purpose; but there is no reason why they should not acquire such training, if facilities were available, particularly at the older Universities. Moreover, the work of masters in applied physical education might be more valuable than it is at present, if it were possible to obtain some knowledge of how to teach games and sports during the undergraduate years. It is a commonplace that the best players of games are not necessarily the best teachers of those games, though they may be very useful in coaching the more brilliant boys in their own particular game or sport, and many masters now arrive at school with undoubted personal skill in some directions, but waste valuable years in acquiring the ability to pass on to the average boy the fundamentals of their particular activity.

For example, the young graduate who is good athlete or swimmer must possess much knowledge of the technique and training required for his particular events, but it does not follow automatically that he has the knowledge necessary to organise athletics or swimming in the school to which he is appointed. For the three or four years when he will have been competing in the adult class, he will have become familiar with methods of coaching rather than methods of teaching, and it is at least probable that he will know little of the subject apart from his own events, and less of its application to the immature body and mind. If he is placed in charge of athletics, he will be expected to know something about all the track and field events which are carried on. If he is put in charge of swimming, he must know something about the modern crawl, back, and breast-strokes, as well as diving and life-saving. Moreover, he will find himself faced with the difficulty of organising athletics or swimming for the whole school, which must include the good, the bad, and the indifferent performers, as well as with the problems connected with sports and house-competitions. Many schools are now in this condition, and, while some masters do spend time and money in acquiring the necessary knowledge to organise well athletics or swimming, it is fatally easy for them to concentrate on the best pupils, and even to produce good teams, but to neglect the great majority. In my opinion, this is nothing less than a prostitution of the purpose of sport in schools; and one of the great advantages of Physical Education is that the abilities of a few outstanding individuals are not unduly emphasised, but that the general level of physical endeavour is raised as high as possible, and the weak are assisted and encouraged to improve.

Now, it would be absurd to suggest that the Universities should strive to produce thoroughly competent coaches; but, for those undergraduates who intend to become school-masters, there should be available some instruction in the teaching of the fundamentals of games, sports, and gymnastics, especially during the fourth or diploma year. Obviously, the training would vary greatly from that required for a definite post as an assistant to a Director, to that necessary to enable a man to help in one branch of Physical Education. With such training, personal skill could be developed into teaching ability, masters would approach the whole subject in a more scientific and understanding spirit, and there would be a great increase in the number of those who could devote a very active attention to some aspect of Physical Education in addition to their academic work.

When Physical Education has been started and its aims and objects understood by the school at large, it provides valuable opportunities for leadership by the boys themselves; but it must be clearly understood that this leadership has very definite limits. In the gymnasium, boys from the lowest to the highest forms may be employed as leaders at suitable moments during the normal lesson, but they are always under the eye of the master. In voluntary work they may be used to teach others vaulting and agility movements, provided that they themselves thoroughly understand the movements, while in swimming and similar activities their teaching is often of great assistance. Nevertheless, except under the stress of special circumstances, boys should not be allowed to take other boys in educational gymnastics, because it is so difficult to teach this work properly. In addition to a thorough knowledge of the theory and practice of educational gymnastics an understanding of many other factors is also needed, and this is quite beyond the capacity of most boys.

So far we have discussed the practical work which is carried on inside and outside the gymnasium and the methods that should be employed in finding the right people to do that work. Now it remains for us to consider what we may call the theoretical side of Physical Education and the means by which the department may foster a good liaison with the academic work and render a valuable contribution to the school as a whole. To begin with, a great deal of thinking and planning has to be done to ensure the smooth running of the practical work already enumerated. The tables which are employed in the gymnastics lesson to-day do not consist of a meaningless and haphazard collection of exercises. I have said that the modern system of educational gymnastics is based on the Swedish system modified by more recent work in Denmark and adapted to suit English schools. It offers a progressive course in movement, the aims of which are health, activity, grace, and strength. Each lesson consists of a table or series of exercises compiled by the master and arranged in a definite order. The table usually begins with some free running or a quick ball-game to stimulate circulation and breathing; then follow several free-standing exercises carried out in class-formation to provide a preliminary warming and suppling of the whole body. After this the stronger localised exercises are introduced, for which apparatus is desirable, and team-work may be employed with advantage. The culmination of the table is reached in jumping, vaulting, and agility work, movements which require the greatest concentration of the mind and free use of the body. The table is normally completed by a quiet exercise or a short period of relaxation and a test of carriage or posture. Progression and grading are of fundamental importance.

Recreational gymnastics, voluntary work, the teaching of athletics, swimming, and other sports all require considerable preparation. In addition to this, it is essential to take regular statistics of physique. Such data form a useful criterion of the progress which is being made from term to term and year to year, and provide a reliable check of the development of the individual or group: houses, forms, or age-groups. To be of value, the data must be taken at sufficiently frequent intervals. Weight should be taken three times per term, during the first week, during the half-term week, and during the last week. Height should be taken twice a term, and chest measurement once a year in December, when the body is most stable. The data must then be assembled and analysed so that they can be used. On entering the public schools a number of boys are found to be suffering from simple physical defects, such as round-shoulders, poking chin, hollow back, flat feet and chest. Moreover, these defects may well make their appearance during school life owing to special stresses of various kinds or to a lack of general physical development. By co-operation with the medical officer, physical examinations can be conducted at sufficiently frequent intervals, and many of these defects may be ameliorated or cured by means of suitable corrective exercises, control of the type or quantity of exercise undertaken, and various other methods.

In my opinion, it would be an excellent thing if some form of theoretical instruction could be allied with practical work. A large number of boys at present grow up in profound ignorance of the structure of their bodies and of the simplest life processes. As things are, it is exceedingly difficult to give more than a glimpse of such matters. If time could be found for a theoretical course, better results would be achieved in practical work and in the correction of bad habits of posture and carriage. It must be remembered that the Director himself takes the whole school; probably he is the only master in such a position, so that from records and his knowledge of the boys he builds up a mass of useful information to be used when required. In addition, his specialist work brings him in touch with child psychology and with hygiene. In schools where an understanding exists between the Director, the headmaster, and other masters, he is often able to give valuable assistance to these masters in dealing with the backward, the troublesome, and the difficult. I do not suggest that the Director should usurp the functions of the School Medical Officer or of outside specialists, but the gap between the Child Guidance Clinic or the Specialist on the one hand, and the ordinary overworked schoolmaster on the other, is wide. Now, the Director should be a schoolmaster who lives with the boys, and his specialist work should make him a valuable link in the chain. In the old days, when schools were less pleasant places than they are now and life was far more strenuous, the nervous, the defective, and the unstable were educated elsewhere. To-day, most schools have a considerable number of boys who are suffering from some emotional or physical maladjustment, and they cannot all be expected to conform to rigid codes of work and conduct all the time. We must be prepared to make some adjustment where necessary, and in this work the Director of Physical Education has an important function to fulfil.

At the beginning I said that I did not propose to define Physical Education as it stands to-day, but I hope I have shown that it differs fundamentally from the Physical Training of the past. Perhaps I may be bold enough now to risk a few generalisations:

Training aims at imposing a technique and is a method of mastering a process; though an essential part of education, it is only a part. Thus, the teaching of a language so as to read or write commercial letters and business publications is a vocational training, whereas learning a language as a means of studying literature and history is more than this—it is an aid to living. A liberal education fosters intelligence and is the source of a principle of integration. We may compare Physical Training with Vocational Training and Physical Education with Education. Physical Training aims at memorising movements, it is a training for movement and a response to an external discipline. Further, it is severely restricted. Physical Education aims at studying movement and is education through movement. It applies to every branch of education in which movement plays a part and includes re-education of those below normal. Physical Training aims at teaching patterns of movement. At its highest Physical Education aims at helping the individual to make his own design for living.

In this address I have pointed out that in schools where true Physical Education is attempted all the physical activities should be co-ordinated and made the subject of careful planning. I have tried to suggest that masters should have more knowledge of the bodies and life-processes of the boys they teach, that a central organisation can be established for the keeping of statistics, both of individuals and of the school as a whole, and I have endeavoured to reveal the need for a fuller understanding of the emotional and environmental difficulties which beset our pupils.

THE RELEVANCE OF EDUCATION TO BEHAVIOUR

S. H. Wood

W HEN I accepted an invitation to give the concluding address at this Conference and was asked to furnish a title to my remarks, I realised that I was faced with two alternatives. I could prepare a speech beforehand, keep clear of your company until the last day and then, appearing as a complete stranger, loose upon you something wholly unrelated to anything that had gone before. Or I could, if I were allowed, listen to the addresses and discussions and then unburden my mind without any particular regard to the title printed on the programme. To have adopted the first alternative would have been an impertinence. I propose therefore to address you without concerning myself whether I shall be dealing, throughout, with the 'relevance of education to behaviour'. I ought, by way of preface, to say that I have not been able to attend every lecture, and that, as I am not a teacher, I shall not presume to talk to you about teaching, though education may keep breaking in.

We have listened to some provocative addresses; and if we have allowed provocation to do its proper work and have not rested at that dead end of 'I accept this and reject that', but have ploughed on with our own thinking, we shall have done some productive work. There is a difference between thinking and good thinking; and anyone who accepts the illumination of Jesus about God and the nature of man is aware of the values by which he must test his thinking to know whether it be good thinking.

Jesus revealed both by His teaching and by His life, which are inseparable, that God is a reality, that man is fashioned in God's likeness, and that the possibility of communion between man and God is a fact of existence. There is another illumination of Jesus which, because it reveals the essential nature of God and therefore the potentiality of man, knits the whole into one fabric. It is that God is not primarily righteousness, justice or peace, but love.

What is our attitude to this affirmation that God is love? As a text, from one of the Epistles, it is still commonly to be found on the walls of modest lodging-houses at seaside resorts, but less commonly on the walls of hotels. It frequently adorns the homes of the humble, but less often those of the prosperous. It is probably the most famous of all sayings, but less and less does it appear to find acceptance in the hearts of men and women; with the result that in our personal, social, and political relationships with our fellows our highest ideal is something we call loyalty. One of the speakers at this Conference said to me some years ago that it was possible for a man to elevate loyalty into a sinister religion. That is true of many kinds of loyalty—loyalty to friends, to church, and to state. But you cannot exalt love into anything but the religion of Jesus. It is convenient but cowardly to sidetrack love by the constant affirmation that it is not emotionalism or sentimentality. It would be more profitable if we reminded ourselves that it suffers long and is kind, and does not behave itself unseemly; and that, though we should covet earnestly the best gifts, love is the more excellent way.

Is the direction and temper of our thinking consistent with this revelation of the worth of the individual, or are we treating men and women as means to some end instead of as an end in themselves? It is not the group, the class, the state or the church, still less is it politics, economics, psychology or theology that is made in the image of God. It is this man, this woman, this boy, this girl who is so made. There was a man of the seventeenth century, Nicholas Herman, better known as Brother Lawrence, whose conversations with God and man, simple and direct, have been collected together under the title 'The Practice of the Presence of God'. If we are lighted by the illumination of which I have been speaking, we know that there must also be a practice of the presence of the individual; and we also know that it is by the values which emerge from these twin practices, inseparable as two sides of a shield, that we must test our thinking and our behaviour.

Traherne, the mystic, put a truth about good thinking with economy and beauty when he said: 'To think well is to serve God in the interior court.' If we add, as we must since we are ordinary men and not mystics, that to behave well is to serve God in the outer court, a purpose of education becomes clear. It is both to encourage good thinking and to break down the barriers which exist between the inner court of thought and the outer court of behaviour so that good thinking may the more freely issue in good behaviour. This alone integrates personal freedom with social responsibility. But freedom has its disadvantages. Schweitzer says: 'Any man who thinks for himself and at the same time is spiritually free is to political, social, and religious organisations something inconvenient and even uncanny.' We do not like to be thought awkward, still less queer. The protection of the herd is softly comforting. And yet a man who would help his fellows in the task of freeing themselves must himself be patiently engaged in becoming master of his own soul and be prepared quietly to bear the inconvenient consequences. Moreover, he must beware of the psychologists. A man is on the way to spiritual freedom when he can say: 'Yes, according to all the best psychological opinion I am, of course, an introvert or an extrovert and, because I had this or that experience in infancy and because I am now encompassed by this or that circumstance, I ought, no doubt, meekly to enter the pigeon hole so carefully prepared for me by the psychologists. But, being a living soul, I decline life in a pigeon hole, because therein I cannot be free neither can I grow.' The variety of pigeon holes prepared for us by different psychologists on the same data is, no doubt, due to the fact that psychologists, too, are living souls.

Are we free either intellectually or spiritually? We are too lazy or too fearful to grapple with germinal or revolutionary ideas. I am not scholar enough to know whether the teaching and life of Jesus were revolutionary to his time, but, try as I will, I cannot escape the realisation that they are revolutionary to my time. When I reflect upon my own thinking in the light of 'Ye cannot serve God and mammon'—'Love your enemies'—'Resist not evil'—'Our Father which art in Heaven'—I know that I have enough revolutionary doctrine to last me a lifetime. If I thought that the Sermon on the Mount was merely a body of moral exhortations I should be in despair. But when I study it as a picture by a supreme artist delineating behaviour which flows from acceptance, without qualification, of kinship with God, I begin to take courage; and courage is fortified when I find that a central figure comes to life in the person of Jesus.

I do not need to be told that Jesus was not a politician, that He did not preach an economic doctrine and that He did not found a church; but it is idle to tell me that He is not a revolutionary. A refusal to accept Him as such means that I am allowing my intellectual arteries to harden and am deliberately engaged in rendering unto Caesar the things that are God's. These reflections lead me to enquire what is the meaning of that episode in the life of Jesus which has been used in the past, and is the more used to-day, to justify some kind of divided allegiance: 'Render therefore unto Caesar the things which are Caesar's: and unto God the things that are God's.' A brilliant rejoinder! But surely more than that. May it not be that the brilliance which disconcerts those who seek to entangle Jesus reveals a divine philosophy to those who are willing to understand Him? If we have allowed any penny of our personality to become stamped with the image and superscription of state, church, politics, power, ambition, lust or pride, there is no alternative for us but to render that coin accordingly. We know that only too well. But do we not also spiritually apprehend that, if we would seek the service which is perfect freedom, so also must we strive to prevent any attachment or loyalty from obscuring in us the image of God? This much, at least, is clear, that Jesus did not say or imply that the penny ought to have been stamped with the image and superscription of Caesar, but only that as it was so stamped its destination was inevitable. I can see in this story a painful explanation of a divided allegiance, but no justification for it. I can see in it a challenge, but no comfortable consolation for our cowardice.

There is another freedom, the lack of which is not within our experience, though it casts a shadow over a large number of our fellows. I mean economic freedom. How smugly we talk about our democracy. It is a sign of good thinking that we distinguish between political democracy and economic democracy. If there were equality of opportunity for the nourishment of the body and for the nurture of the mind, there would be no conference of young public school masters. Bernard Shaw, whose intellectual freedom seems to make him delight in being inconvenient, said thirty years ago—before some of you were born—that every gentleman knew that what was the matter with the poor was their poverty; yet that we did not mean to abolish poverty, but only to breed a race of people who would not notice it.

I sometimes have to expound the English educational system to foreigners, and when I have described the grant-aided secondary schools with their obligation to admit 'children of the poor', free if need be, and have then gone on to explain those other secondary schools known as 'the public schools', there is generally a pause. After a while there comes the question: 'Is there any class consciousness in your country?' At one time I found that question difficult to answer, but experience has taught me to reply: 'No, not much; class divisions are so deep that we are scarcely conscious of them.' The members of this conference belong to a privileged class and are engaged in educating boys who belong to the same privileged class—the class with economic freedom.

If, so far, I have not dealt directly with the relevance of education to behaviour, I will devote the remainder of my remarks broadly to that subject. We spend about a hundred million pounds a year on education. What are the results of the work and care of the men and women who earn their bread and butter in the schools? No one can answer that question accurately because human behaviour, with which education is concerned, is not subject to quantitative measurement. Nor will I attempt a qualitative judgment. Instead, I will suggest three tests of an educated man. And to avoid too much impersonality I will address the tests to you; as I have in the past frequently addressed them to myself, with disastrous results. Do you know how to entertain a new idea? Do you know how to entertain the other person? Do you know how to entertain yourself?

Do you know how to entertain a new idea? When a new idea comes to meet you do you brace yourself for the battle or do you slink round the corner? Do you, in vulgar language, rag the life out of it, toss it to and fro with your friends and then, if it be false or tawdry, reject it? But if the battle leads to good thinking do you determine to readjust your attitude to life in the light of anything real that you have got out of it? That is the pursuit of truth.

Do you know how to entertain the other person? He may be richer or poorer, less stupid or more stupid, blacker or yellower. He may be the man next door, or the more distant miner sweating for his own economic security and for your comfort, or the still more distant coolie or native so liable to exploitation in the alleged interests of Western civilisation. Do you behave generously to him either directly or through social and political institutions? Are you a devotee of the art of good human relations? That is the pursuit of goodness.

Do you know how to entertain yourself? When removed from the clash of intellectual battles and remote from the company of your fellows, do you know how to occupy yourself? Are you an artist or craftsman, however humble, or can you lose yourself in appreciation of the works of those who are? Have you an inner life that does not require the ministrations of others? This is, ultimately, the pursuit of beauty; and I doubt whether you can make any greater contribution to the serenity of a troubled world than to usher from school to life young people who not only are able to sustain a measure of loneliness but seek it.

It is on this question of meditation that I wish to close. Some of us may doubt whether this so-called communion with God is anything more than an ascetic mental exercise. Aldous Huxley in his book *Ends and Means* says, 'men cannot realise their unity with others and with ultimate reality unless they practice the virtues of love and understanding', but on the same page he remarks that 'ultimate reality is impersonal and non-ethical'. If you read the passage in full you may wonder what has happened to his main thesis that means determine ends. But, apart from this, it appears to me that Huxley arrives at his conclusion about the impersonality of ultimate reality, partly, at any rate, from a study of the mystics. If God be personal I should not expect that discovery inevitably to be made by those who withdraw themselves from persons, but rather by men and women whose meditative life embraces the constant search for God in their fellows. I dare not attempt any further exposition. But I am impelled to offer you this. There stands out in my experience one friend who combined a deep and lonely life of contemplation with a surpassing love for men and women. I speak with restraint when I say that I do not think Canon Sheppard apprehended God as impersonal.

'Ultimate reality' is a philosophical term, and, if it can be properly described as impersonal, I can only hazard the conjecture that God transcends even philosophy; and that possibly the most significant happening for this distracted but redeemable world is that, once upon a time, the 'Word was made flesh and dwelt among us full of grace and truth'.

APPENDIX

BROADCASTING AND EDUCATION

A. C. Cameron, M.C., M.A.

BROADCASTING is not just a convenient classroom aid. It is part of the home background of young people in every walk of life, and its use in school to-day is one of the various ways in which we are able to link up home interests with school life; and in return for this interest the school can, and I believe ought, to do something to guide the listening of its boys. For long enough it has been accepted as a part of education to guide children's taste in reading and in music. I believe we owe it to the coming generation to give them some guidance in how to use the two new mediums, broadcasting and the cinema.

I am not seeking to impose my own, or anybody else's, taste on them. I do not want to make any boy listen to talks, who would rather listen to swing music. But I do want to see him make a choice. The worst misuse of broadcasting to-day is what has been well described as tap-listening. The tap is left running all day, and nobody pays much attention to the indeterminate background of sound which comes out of it. The very fact of listening in school seriously to good broadcasts may not only help to train boys in selective listening at home, but also teach them to listen in school to their masters. That at least has been the experience of many teachers to whom I have spoken.

But let me turn to the classroom, because, after all, however closely you may agree with what I have said in general, you as schoolmasters, if you use broadcasting, will be working with it mainly in that sphere. There in effect you will be introducing a new personality between your form and yourself. That is a dangerous thing to do if the broadcast is allowed to play directly on the class and the master does nothing. A successful broadcast depends on activity at both ends: at the microphone someone with something to say which is worth saying and the power to express himself brings his experience of life to the microphone; and the schoolmaster takes the material and shapes it to his particular needs. You and I, for example, may be listening to the same broadcast, but in different parts of the country and with different types of children. The use we make of it, the type of our follow-up, may be quite different but equally suited to our particular needs. The test of a good broadcast is whether or not it gives something which the teacher cannot give. The answer to this question will vary with the needs of the form and the experience of the master: hence the wide range of material provided in our programme.

What is that material? Among the talks designed specially for secondary schools there are the Modern Language broadcasts, junior and senior series; talks on Music for the Coming Week; the Sixth Form Talks; and also the Church History series on Monday mornings, which though not regarded strictly as school broadcasting has the sixth forms of public and secondary schools particularly in mind. In addition, there are series, as in History, Geography, and Biology, which are arranged primarily for the senior elementary schools (that is for schools with non-specialist teachers), but which are also widely taken in secondary schools; as, indeed, are some of the courses classified junior, such as Travel Talks and Nature Study.

I should explain here briefly our organisation. The B.B.C. has handed over to the Central Council for School Broadcasting (an independent body representing educationists, teachers, and administrators) responsibility for the educational content and design of the courses it broadcasts. Under the Council effective control is in the hands of committees consisting of serving teachers and of subject specialists, so that those who are to use the broadcasts are effectively in charge of their arrangement; and in the series such as the Sciences, which are mainly intended for the elementary schools, there are also representatives of secondary schools on the committee.

Outside the special schools programme, there is the general programme, various items of which from time to time are of interest to secondary schools. We try to call attention to such items in various ways, as for instance in the Senior Modern Language pamphlets, and I know that in many schools guidance is given both as to home and as to unofficial school listening.

I do not suppose many of your people listen to the Children's Hour, and, though I hope some interesting experiments may be made in the near future in designing talks addressed particularly to young people in their teens, the main focus of interest in the general programme of which I want to speak is the series of talks for Discussion Groups in the evening programme, all of which fall within the period 7.30–9.0 p.m., and some of which in the past have, I know, been found of interest to public schools.

I do not mean to suggest that either in school or at home the boy who wants to be a selective listener need necessarily join a Discussion Group: he may prefer to listen by himself to music or foreign affairs, or to whatever it may be. But those people of any age who want to use the traditional method of adult education—i.e. group discussion—can get it from the contribution which the Corporation makes to adult education. Three series each term are designed with the needs of Group Listening particularly in mind. But these talks are in a somewhat different category to those designed for use in school. The 'programme value' of the evening times, when they are given, is such that the Corporation has to have regard also to the needs of the general listener; but, subject to that, the organisation of Group Discussion has been handed over by the Corporation to another independent body, the Central Committee for Group Listening. And that body is freely consulted as to the content and arrangement of the talks.

So much for the main lines. Now let me turn to points of special difficulty. I know the first of these in your mind is the timing of the courses, the majority of which are given in the afternoon. Our present time-table is based on the needs of the day school because it was drawn up at a time when, frankly, boarding schools were not taking much notice of broadcasting. I realise in particular that many of you are now wanting to take the Sixth Form Talks, but that you find the present hour, viz. 3.35 p.m. on Friday, impossible for boarding schools. I can only say that the B.B.C. has this problem under review and recognises that the needs of the public schools must now be taken into account together with those of other types of schools, and I hope it may be possible to make some modifications in the programme.

Then there is the question of syllabus. If the difficulty of the timing of the series is overcome, are you able to use weekly talks in, say, Regional Geography, or do you find that a weekly talk with the preparation and follow-up takes up more time than you can afford to devote to it while you are carrying on your own syllabus independently? Would you prefer fortnightly talks, or do those of you who have used our series as complete courses find that in effect it is possible, without undue dislocation of your own syllabus, to merge the two schemes into one? Or, again, do you prefer to pick individual broadcasts out of the series? This is possible in most of them; indeed, they are arranged with that end in view.

May I refer, too, to the possible use with older and slower pupils of courses like Travel Talks and Nature Study, originally designed for juniors? I believe myself that this is a perfectly proper thing to do. These series are so arranged that, while sufficiently simple in matter for juniors, they are not too immature for rather older boys.

Then there is the question of suitability of material: can the same series be equally suitable to a senior elementary school which has no specialist teacher in your sense of the term, and to you who have? It has been suggested, and I think this may be the right answer, that the same material may be suitable to both, but will be used differently. The specialist will use it for revision and the non-specialist much more as the basic material of his course. There is a further and perhaps more far-reaching difficulty: will the needs of the boy of thirteen who has to leave school at fourteen be found to be the same as those of the boy of thirteen who will be going on to the University?

The General Programme may be recommended for use by forms or discussion groups, and suggestions as to its contents will always be welcomed at the B.B.C. Such help will also be useful in enabling the illustrated pamphlets to be improved.

A good deal of the benefit of talks is lost without the pamphlets. Broadcasting depends on the spoken word for creating its impression and, as you know, it is remarkable how clear a visual picture can be built up simply by words. But to help in this process and to give both a focus for the pupil's attention and an illustration of forms with which he may be unfamiliar (e.g. a mangrove tree in tropical Africa), illustrated pamphlets are provided with most of the series. These pamphlets contain, in addition to the pictures, suggestions for further reading and for follow-up for each talk. They are intended for the pupil, but also may be found of service to the teacher, particularly to him who, in a small school, is trying to cover a subject which is not really his own.

The cinema is often discussed in connection with broadcasting, and it is sometimes suggested that the two are opposed, that they are in some sense rivals. That, I think, is quite untrue. They are concerned with different things. The essence of one is sound, and of the other, sight. They are really complementary and I am hoping that some more work may be done by schools interested in using visual apparatus in conjunction with broadcasting, and I should be much interested to hear of any experimental work on these lines.

In conclusion, I would emphasise that the appreciation of the finer values of broadcasting, particularly in language talks, where the quality of the spoken word is particularly important, reception must be good. Without it, there is bound to be disappointment. One of the services that the Corporation has rendered to education is the loan of a body of expert engineers who are always prepared to give advice on particular problems of reception and of installation.

INDEX

For EU product safety concerns, contact us at Calle de José Abascal, 56–1°,
28003 Madrid, Spain or eugpsr@cambridge.org.

www.ingramcontent.com/pod-product-compliance
Ingram Content Group UK Ltd.
Pitfield, Milton Keynes, MK11 3LW, UK
UKHW012341130625
459647UK00009B/452